W9-BVJ-566

Gun Control

Opposing Viewpoints®

WAGGONER LIB
Trevecca Nazarene University
DISCARD

David L. Bender, *Publisher*

Bruno Leone, *Executive Editor*

Scott Barbour, *Managing Editor*

Brenda Stalcup, *Senior Editor*

Tamara L. Roleff, *Book Editor*

OPPOSING VIEWPOINTS® SERIES

MACKEY LIBRAR
Trevecca Nazarene Universi

Greenhaven Press, Inc., San Diego, California

Cover photo: Photodisc

Library of Congress Cataloging-in-Publication Data

Gun control : opposing viewpoints / Tamara L. Roleff, book editor.
    p.   cm. — (Opposing viewpoints series)
    Includes bibliographical references and index.
    ISBN 1-56510-663-6 (lib. bdg. : alk. paper). —
ISBN 1-56510-662-8 (pbk. : alk. paper)
    1. Gun control—United States. 2. Firearms ownership—United
States. I. Roleff, Tamara L., 1959–   . II. Series: Opposing viewpoints
series (Unnumbered)
HV7436.G868 1997
363.3'3'0973—dc21   96-48029
                                                                                              CIP

Copyright ©1997 by Greenhaven Press, Inc.
Printed in the U.S.A.

No part of this book may be reproduced or used in any form or by any
means, electrical, mechanical, or otherwise, including, but not limited
to, photocopy, recording, or any information storage and retrieval
system, without prior written permission from the publisher.

Every effort has been made to trace the owners of copyrighted material.

Greenhaven Press, Inc., P.O. Box 289009
San Diego, CA 92198-9009

Gun Control

Opposing Viewpoints®

OTHER BOOKS OF RELATED INTEREST

OPPOSING VIEWPOINTS SERIES

America's Cities
America's Prisons
Civil Liberties
Crime and Criminals
Criminal Justice
The Death Penalty
Gangs
Juvenile Crime
The Legal System
Sexual Violence
Violence

CURRENT CONTROVERSIES SERIES

Drug Trafficking
Family Violence
Gun Control
Urban Terrorism
Violence Against Women
Youth Violence

AT ISSUE SERIES

Domestic Violence
The Jury System
The Militia Movement

"CONGRESS SHALL MAKE NO LAW...ABRIDGING THE FREEDOM OF SPEECH, OR OF THE PRESS."

First Amendment to the U.S. Constitution

The basic foundation of our democracy is the First Amendment guarantee of freedom of expression. The Opposing Viewpoints Series is dedicated to the concept of this basic freedom and the idea that it is more important to practice it than to enshrine it.

CONTENTS

WHY CONSIDER
OPPOSING VIEWPOINTS?

"The only way in which a human being can make some approach to knowing the whole of a subject is by hearing what can be said about it by persons of every variety of opinion and studying all modes in which it can be looked at by every character of mind. No wise man ever acquired his wisdom in any mode but this."

John Stuart Mill

In our media-intensive culture it is not difficult to find differing opinions. Thousands of newspapers and magazines and dozens of radio and television talk shows resound with differing points of view. The difficulty lies in deciding which opinion to agree with and which "experts" seem the most credible. The more inundated we become with differing opinions and claims, the more essential it is to hone critical reading and thinking skills to evaluate these ideas. Opposing Viewpoints books address this problem directly by presenting stimulating debates that can be used to enhance and teach these skills. The varied opinions contained in each book examine many different aspects of a single issue. While examining these conveniently edited opposing views, readers can develop critical thinking skills such as the ability to compare and contrast authors' credibility, facts, argumentation styles, use of persuasive techniques, and other stylistic tools. In short, the Opposing Viewpoints Series is an ideal way to attain the higher-level thinking and reading skills so essential in a culture of diverse and contradictory opinions.

In addition to providing a tool for critical thinking, Opposing Viewpoints books challenge readers to question their own strongly held opinions and assumptions. Most people form their opinions on the basis of upbringing, peer pressure, and personal, cultural, or professional bias. By reading carefully balanced opposing views, readers must directly confront new ideas as well as the opinions of those with whom they disagree. This is not to simplistically argue that everyone who reads opposing views will—or should—change his or her opinion. Instead, the series enhances readers' understanding of their own views by encouraging confrontation with opposing ideas. Careful examination of others' views can lead to the readers' understanding of the logical inconsistencies in their own opinions, perspective on why they hold an opinion, and the consideration of the possibility that their opinion requires further evaluation.

EVALUATING OTHER OPINIONS

To ensure that this type of examination occurs, Opposing Viewpoints books present all types of opinions. Prominent spokespeople on different sides of each issue as well as well-known professionals from many disciplines challenge the reader. An additional goal of the series is to provide a forum for other, less known, or even unpopular viewpoints. The opinion of an ordinary person who has had to make the decision to cut off life support from a terminally ill relative, for example, may be just as valuable and provide just as much insight as a medical ethicist's professional opinion. The editors have two additional purposes in including these less known views. One, the editors encourage readers to respect others' opinions—even when not enhanced by professional credibility. It is only by reading or listening to and objectively evaluating others' ideas that one can determine whether they are worthy of consideration. Two, the inclusion of such viewpoints encourages the important critical thinking skill of objectively evaluating an author's credentials and bias. This evaluation will illuminate an author's reasons for taking a particular stance on an issue and will aid in readers' evaluation of the author's ideas.

As series editors of the Opposing Viewpoints Series, it is our hope that these books will give readers a deeper understanding of the issues debated and an appreciation of the complexity of even seemingly simple issues when good and honest people disagree. This awareness is particularly important in a democratic society such as ours in which people enter into public debate to determine the common good. Those with whom one disagrees should not be regarded as enemies but rather as people whose views deserve careful examination and may shed light on one's own.

Thomas Jefferson once said that "difference of opinion leads to inquiry, and inquiry to truth." Jefferson, a broadly educated man, argued that "if a nation expects to be ignorant and free . . . it expects what never was and never will be." As individuals and as a nation, it is imperative that we consider the opinions of others and examine them with skill and discernment. The Opposing Viewpoints Series is intended to help readers achieve this goal.

David L. Bender & Bruno Leone,
Series Editors

INTRODUCTION

> "Guns don't kill, people do."
>
> National Rifle Association slogan

> "Guns don't die, people do."
>
> Pete Shields and John Greenya,
> Guns Don't Die—People Do

One night in November 1994, Bobby and Tilda Crabtree were visiting Bobby's sister when their fourteen-year-old daughter Kaye telephoned. She would be staying the night at a friend's house, she said. Kaye's father was glad she had checked in so he would not have to worry about her. Just a few days earlier, someone had thrown a brick through the Crabtrees' front window, and a neighbor had recently been kidnapped, raped, and left for dead. So when the Crabtree family returned to their home in Monroe, Louisiana, and heard noises coming from a bedroom closet upstairs, they were certain it was a burglar. Bobby Crabtree got his .357 magnum and went to investigate. He went to the bedroom, turned on the light, listened for more noise, then walked to the closet door. When he yanked open the door, two people jumped out at him, yelling. Instinctively, he fired, only to discover that the "burglars" were his daughter and her friend, playing a prank. The bullet from Crabtree's gun entered Kaye's neck; she died twelve hours later.

Gun-control advocates argue that Kaye Crabtree's death was an accident that would never have happened if gun ownership were more strictly controlled, while gun-control opponents maintain that such accidents, while regrettable, are rare. Those who support strict gun laws believe accidental shootings like Kaye's are inevitable when private citizens are easily able to acquire guns. Josh Sugarmann, founder of the Violence Policy Center, an educational foundation that researches gun violence, maintains that firearms are more likely to be used against the guns' owners, families, and acquaintances than against violent criminals. He asserts that guns provide the opportunity for angry disagreements and impulsive fights to turn into deadly attacks. According to the 1994 report "Cease Fire: A Comprehensive Strategy to Reduce Firearms Violence" by Sugarmann and Kristen Rand, 29 percent of the murders in 1992 stemmed from arguments. In addition, they write, in those 1992 murders in which the relationship between the murder victim and offender was known to researchers, more than three times as many people were killed by a relative or acquaintance than by a stranger.

Gun-control advocates also maintain that guns are an ineffective means of self-defense. Sugarmann and Rand cite medical studies that have found that a person who keeps a gun in the home is three times more likely than someone who does not own a gun to be murdered by a family member or acquaintance. They also point to the FBI finding that in 1992 there were only 262 instances of justifiable homicide with a firearm—using a gun to kill someone in self-defense. Supporters of gun control assert that in the vast majority of violent crimes, people are unable to successfully defend themselves with their guns and may even increase the danger to themselves and others. For instance, in 1993 Colin Ferguson shot a number of commuters on the Long Island Rail Road before being subdued. A former law enforcement officer and Vietnam veteran who was wounded by Ferguson testified at a congressional hearing in March 1995 that he would not have been able to save any lives if he had been carrying a gun.

> There is no question in my mind that I would have done more damage if I had possessed such a weapon than the six deaths and the nineteen injuries that occurred on the train. . . . And with people running and knocking one another down, if someone behind me had started firing, I dare say I would then think I was in a crossfire.

The confusion and panic among the train's passengers were so great, he asserted, that the possibility that he or any other passenger could have killed Ferguson with a single well-aimed shot was highly unlikely.

Opponents of gun control maintain, however, that handguns are an effective means of self-defense. Many gun owners have testified before Congress that their handguns have protected them from harm by intruders and other criminals. Others, such as Suzanna Gratia Hupp—whose parents were among the twenty-three people killed in October 1991 when George Hennard opened fire in Luby's Cafeteria in Killeen, Texas—believe innocent lives have been lost due to existing firearms regulations. Hupp, an accomplished shooter, has testified several times before Congress that if she had brought her gun into Luby's instead of leaving it in her car so as not to break Texas's law against carrying concealed weapons, she would have been able to stop Hennard before he killed her parents and other customers. "I had a clear shot at him," she asserts.

Gun-control opponents argue that studies that purport to show the dangers of gun ownership do not take into account the benefits of gun ownership. Edgar A. Suter, a physician and founder of Doctors for Integrity in Research and Public Policy, contends that the benefits of gun ownership should be measured not by how many burglars and rapists are killed, but by how many lives are saved, injuries and medical costs prevented, and properties protected. Suter and others who oppose gun control maintain that research that only counts how many people are killed is flawed because it does not include cases in which intruders or attackers are wounded or frightened off by a gun. If these instances are taken into account, they assert, the effectiveness of guns for self-defense increases dramatically.

Criminologists, law enforcement officers, researchers, and gun-control advocates and opponents all cite evidence to support their positions on the benefits or drawbacks of efforts to limit gun ownership. *Gun Control: Opposing Viewpoints* presents their arguments in the following chapters: Does Private Ownership of Handguns Pose a Serious Threat to Society? Does the Constitution Protect Private Gun Ownership? Is Gun Ownership an Effective Means of Self-Defense? What Measures Would Reduce Gun Violence? This anthology examines the tension that arises when the desire to ensure public safety clashes with the need to protect individual rights.

CHAPTER 1

DOES PRIVATE OWNERSHIP OF HANDGUNS POSE A SERIOUS THREAT TO SOCIETY?

CHAPTER PREFACE

With two hundred million guns in circulation and another fifteen thousand manufactured every day, there are enough firearms to arm nearly every man, woman, and child in the United States. Gun-control advocates contend that this proliferation of guns is behind America's crime rate—the highest among industrialized nations. Reduce the number of guns available, they assert, and the crime rate will go down. To support their contention, they cite a study by the National Institute of Justice in Kansas City, Missouri, known as the Kansas City Gun Experiment. During a six-month trial period from July 1992 through January 1993, the Kansas City police increased their patrols in one of the city's worst crime areas with the goal of confiscating illegally carried guns. The study found that when the number of illegally carried guns confiscated by the police rose by 65 percent, gun crime dropped by 49 percent. Neighboring areas in which patrols were not increased did not experience any significant changes in the crime rate during the same period.

Critics of the Kansas City Gun Experiment argue that many variables could explain the drop in the gun-crime rate in the targeted area. The 65 percent increase in the number of illegally carried guns confiscated by the police amounted to a total of twenty-nine guns, the critics maintain, hardly a significant number in a city where an estimated one hundred thousand handguns are in circulation. Moreover, they theorize that those individuals who were arrested for illegally carrying guns may have accounted for a significant percentage of the area's gun crime. The fact that these criminals were incarcerated for several months may be the primary reason behind the drop in the gun-crime rate, they contend.

For every study gun-control advocates use to show that gun ownership increases the crime rate, gun-rights supporters point to another one that finds gun ownership has the opposite effect. The influence of gun ownership on crime is just one of the issues debated by the authors in the following chapter.

"Every two years, more *Americans*
are killed by guns at home than
were killed in all the years of the
Vietnam war."

PRIVATE OWNERSHIP OF HANDGUNS LEADS TO HIGHER RATES OF GUN VIOLENCE

Claire Safran

The American city of Seattle and the Canadian city of Vancouver
have similar populations, economies, and crime rates, except for
the rates of murder and assault by handguns. In the following
viewpoint, Claire Safran reports that in Seattle, where handguns
are readily available, residents are much more likely to be injured
or murdered with a gun than in Vancouver, where guns are
tightly restricted and difficult to obtain. Seattle's higher rate of
crimes and accidents involving firearms is due to laxer restrictions
on gun ownership, she contends. Safran is a freelance writer.

As you read, consider the following questions:

1. How much more likely is it that someone will be assaulted or
   murdered with a gun in Seattle as opposed to Vancouver,
   according to the *New England Journal of Medicine* study cited by
   the author?
2. What evidence does Safran present to support her contention
   that courses in firearm safety, such as those taught by the
   National Rifle Association, do not reduce gun violence?
3. How many gun injuries were seen in Vancouver hospitals in
   1992 compared with Seattle hospitals, according to Safran?

Claire Safran, "A Tale of Two Cities—and the Difference Guns Make." Reprinted from
Good Housekeeping, November 1993, by permission. Copyright ©1993 by Claire Safran.

"Did I kiss her good-bye that morning? I can't remember." Over and over, Jenny Wieland relives the events of November 20, 1992. She was rushing off to work in Seattle, Wash.; her one and only child, Amy, just 17, was getting ready for school. "Did I tell her that I loved her? Oh, I hope so." It was the last chance she would ever have.

That afternoon, Amy stopped by a friend's apartment. After a while, a 19-year-old boy arrived, high on cheap wine and waving a .38-caliber revolver. "Just fooling around," he said, holding it to Amy's blonde head. Alarmed, she told him to stop, then tried to push the gun away. And then the gun exploded.

Amy never regained consciousness. She died in the hospital the next day. The boy who killed her so carelessly? He was sentenced to three-and-a-half years in prison.

Amy Ragan (her parents were divorced, and she kept her father's name) was a spirited, popular young girl who won blue ribbons at horse shows. Her mother buried her in her favorite clothes—jeans, Western shirt, silver belt buckle, and cowboy hat. Her grandmother placed a red rose in her hands. "I was supposed to see my daughter graduate from high school," says Jenny. "I was supposed to see her get married and have babies. But a boy with a handgun ended it all."

The argument over gun control comes down to this: one gun death at a time, 93 of them every day, more than 34,000 gunshot deaths every year (and most of those deaths—24,000—by handgun), according to FBI statistics. For teenagers like Amy, gun injuries are now an epidemic, the second leading cause of death among young people. According to a 1993 Louis Harris poll, one American parent in five personally knows a child who's been shot.

A TALE OF TWO CITIES

In Vancouver, Canada—just a scenic, three-hour drive from Jenny Wieland's home—the terrible numbers change. Far fewer people live and die by the gun. Scientists have been studying the reasons for that difference, but parents like Maggie Burtinshaw know them by heart. Her son was just 19 when he was gunned down in Vancouver by a 13-year-old boy who, as he told the police, was acting out a plot he'd seen on TV. The boy hid in a department store until after dark, then stole two rifles from an unlocked case and fired them both at the first person he saw, Maggie's son, Eddie.

But that was 1974. Maggie mourned—and then she got moving. "I didn't want it to happen to another mother's son," she says. She lobbied and worked hard with the Vancouver chapter of her country's Coalition for Gun Control. By 1978, tough new laws were in effect. Since then, gun deaths have gone down in Canada . . . but not in the United States.

Sisters in sorrow, Jenny and Maggie live in sister cities, as alike as any two large cities can be. Seattle and Vancouver sit on opposite sides of the U.S.-Canadian border, but they share a common geography, climate, language, and history. They resemble each other more than they do other cities in their own countries. Seattle is safer and more peaceful than most big cities in the United States; Vancouver has a higher rate of violence than most other Canadian cities.

Reprinted with special permission of King Features Syndicate, Inc.

Both are large Pacific ports. Both are famous for their physical beauty and excellent quality of life. Their residents have similar levels of schooling and similar family incomes. Both are overwhelmingly white cities, with black and Hispanic minorities in Seattle and Asian minorities in Vancouver. They share many cultural values and interests. Residents of both cities have a fondness for coffee bars, and they even watch the same TV shows.

But there is a life-and-death difference. According to a seven-year study published in the *New England Journal of Medicine* in 1988, you are almost eight times as likely to be assaulted with a gun in Seattle and five times as likely to be murdered with one.

A team of scientists—led by Dr. John Henry Sloan of the Harborview Medical Center in Seattle—put the two cities under a microscope. The economies, the demographics, the daily behavior of people were too similar to explain the difference in the death toll. One possible cause after another was eliminated, until the researchers were left with only one plausible explanation: Guns are reasonably restricted in Vancouver, but they are out of control in Seattle.

As the cities go, so do the two nations. In the United States, one in two homes has at least one gun in it; in Canada, it's one in four. Canada has not been disarmed; its citizens own hunting rifles and shotguns at about the same rate as Americans. Under a strict law, though, Canadians own only one-tenth as many handguns, the weapons that can be hidden in purse or pocket, the weapons that target and kill more people than any other. In 1992, Canada also put stiff restrictions on military-style assault weapons; only four American states have similar laws. In the U.S., the homicide rate is 9.8 per 100,000 people; that's three-and-a-half times the Canadian murder rate of 2.8 per 100,000.

THE THREAT FROM ANGRY DRIVERS

In Seattle, Cynthia Coston knows all too well what the U.S. numbers mean. On the spring night of April 17, 1993, she was driving home with two sleepy little daughters in the back seat. Her path was blocked by a black Mustang that was stopped in the middle of the road. She waited, unable to pass, and then she honked her horn.

When the Mustang finally moved, turning a corner, Cynthia drove on. She didn't see the 9mm semiautomatic pistol that was being aimed at her car. She did hear the odd, popping noises—"like firecrackers," she thought at first. But then, in the rearview mirror, she saw Loetta, just turned nine, slumped down. Pulling over, scrambling into the back seat, she gasped at the small hole in her daughter's temple, made by a bullet that had come through the back window. "Dear God," the mother prayed. While a passerby phoned for help, she held the dying child in her arms.

To everyone who knew her, Loetta was "a special little girl," lively and curious, with saucer eyes and a megawatt grin. To those who are keeping count, she was the second child to be shot in Seattle that year by someone who was angered or threatened by the simple honking of a car horn.

In Vancouver, Sandra Wahlgren is also the mother of two little children. Happily, she visits the local parks and drives around town with them. She shudders at the Coston tragedy—she has always worried about the firepower across the border. "For years," she says, "we've been warned not to honk our horns when we go to Seattle. Because a driver might get angry. And in Seattle, he might have a gun."

If Vancouver feels safer than Seattle, it is not because its people are naturally more peaceable or law-abiding. The two cities have similar rates of burglaries, robberies, and simple assaults; similar rates of arrests and similar punishments for criminals. They have almost identical rates of aggravated assaults with knives, blunt instruments, or fists. But Seattle's assault rate soars when you add in its much higher number of assaults with guns. In the same way, the two cities have similar rates of murder by various means—until you count the fivefold higher risk of being killed by one of Seattle's easily available handguns.

PUNCTURED MYTHS

The twin-city figures puncture one of the many myths about guns. Groups like the powerful National Rifle Association (NRA) often argue that guns don't kill people; people kill people. They insist that if would-be attackers don't have guns, they will come at you with some other weapons. But the figures show that that isn't happening in Vancouver. Even if it were to happen, citizens would still be safer; a shooting is five times more likely to be fatal than a stabbing.

In Vancouver, guns are hard to come by. There's a 28-day waiting period for a Firearms Acquisition Certificate that allows you to buy rifles and other long guns, and additional stiff requirements for "restricted weapons" like handguns. "The more we restrict handguns, the better off we are," says Gordon Campbell, mayor of Vancouver. "Anyone who thinks we need a free flow of guns just doesn't understand how modern society works."

In Seattle, Mayor Norm Rice also supports gun control. But here, there's only a five-day waiting period for a quick background check. To buy a handgun, you're supposed to be 21 or older, but that hasn't stopped the teenagers of that city. More than one in three Seattle high school students—according to a 1992 *Journal of the American Medical Association* survey by Drs. Charles Callahan and Frederick Rivara—say they have easy access to handguns. (Nationally, according to a Harvard School of Public Health survey, the figures are even more explosive; 59 percent of U.S. children in sixth through twelfth grades say they "could get a handgun if they wanted one.") In Seattle, 11 percent of the boys say they own their own handgun, and one-third of those gun owners admit they've fired at another human being. The young handgun owners are not just gang members, drug users, or school troublemakers. Many of them are "nice kids."

THE COST OF 200 MILLION FIREARMS

Every year, more than 24,000 Americans are killed with handguns in homicides, suicides and accidents. In 1990, 37,155 people died from firearm wounds in the U.S. compared to 13 firearm deaths in Sweden, 91 in Switzerland, 87 in Japan, 68 in Canada, and 22 in Great Britain. The difference is that an estimated 200 million firearms are owned by private citizens in the U.S., including 67 million handguns manufactured for the sole purpose of killing people.

Tim Wheeler, *People's Weekly World*, December 18, 1993.

In Seattle, Joanne Wallace still mourns the day her son Gregg, 15, went out to play in the park with seven of those nice boys. Two of his friends had each filched a handgun from home. They passed the guns from hand to hand. Then one of the boys, just 13, the son of a minister, put a bullet in his .22 caliber pistol. He pulled back the hammer and shot at Gregg. "I just wanted to scare him," he said later. But his aim was deadly, and Gregg, hit in the chest, died almost instantly.

The shooter was sentenced to just eight weeks in juvenile detention. His father, despite Joanne Wallace's pleas to the judge, was not held responsible. "What's a minister doing with guns?" the grieving mother asks. "What's anyone doing with them?" She's now working for a law that already exists in a few other states, a law that would hold parents responsible for a gun that's not kept safely and falls into the hands of a child.

Instead of a law, gun groups like the NRA argue for training in firearms safety. But the boy who shot Gregg had taken such a course. "I'd like to tell people, 'Don't do it. Don't touch that gun,'" he said recently. "But I don't know if they'd listen."

FATAL GUN STATISTICS

His own parents may not be listening. They still believe "responsible people" have a sacred right to own handguns, though they say people with children should "think twice." They, too, knew all the safety rules but, as a recent study shows, people who've been through a training course aren't any more likely than others to keep their guns safely unloaded and securely locked up.

The minister and his family have become part of a fatal gun

statistic. According to a University of Washington study by Drs. Arthur Kellerman and Donald Reay, if there is a gun in the home, it is 43 times more likely to be used to kill its owner, a member of the family, or a friend than to kill an intruder. Some people own guns for sport, some for self-protection. Yet out of the 34,000 gun deaths in America each year, fewer than 300 are listed as "justifiable homicide," the only category that could include shooting a burglar, mugger, or rapist.

Gun fans don't like those figures. They argue that they don't include the large numbers of private citizens whose lives were saved because the intruder or attacker was scared off by a gun. That's true. They also don't include the people—innocent citizens or guilty burglars and rapists—who are wounded by guns. For every gun death, there are four to 10 gun injuries.

The wounded and the maimed are rushed to emergency rooms. In Vancouver, it could be the one at Vancouver General Hospital, but gun injuries are a rare event there. When Dr. Ron Walls checked the records, he found only a dozen for all 1992.

In a Seattle emergency room, they might see that many in a week. "It's not uncommon to see a number of shootings in a single day," reports Chris Martin, nurse-manager for the Emergency Trauma Center at Harborview Medical Center in Seattle. "They come day and night now. They are the innocent and the not-so-innocent."

Among Harborview's recent patients was a young man named Isaac Rollins. On June 1, 1993, he was showing off his new semiautomatic pistol. The handgun made his girlfriend nervous, and he wanted to demonstrate to her how safe it was. He handed her the loaded clip, then pointed the gun at his own head. But there was still a bullet in the chamber, and when he pulled the trigger, it entered his brain.

Miraculously, he survived and is recovering. Still, gun injuries are expensive for all of us. The overall cost to the American health-care system is $4 billion a year. Everyone pays for it in taxes or increased insurance costs or dollars not spent on other health care.

THE REAL ENEMY

In Seattle, one horror story follows another. An attorney is gunned down in his office by an angry husband, taking revenge for a divorce settlement he didn't like. After an argument, a neighbor opens fire on the family next door, killing the mother, wounding the father, and leaving a three-year-old boy paralyzed. A pharmacist, Evelyn Benson, holds the record for staring down the barrel of a gun—her pharmacy has been subjected to 29 armed robberies.

The unknown criminal frightens us, but he may not be the real enemy. A growing body of research shows that the majority of murder victims are not killed by strangers intent on committing a crime; instead, the trigger is pulled by someone they know. And that's especially true of women.

In recent years, more and more women have been arming themselves. The world seems more violent, the streets more dangerous, and gun manufacturers have appealed to that growing fear. They have targeted women as a new market, producing guns that are smaller, even prettier, and advertising some of them as "dishwasher safe." Yet according to another study by Dr. Kellerman, sponsored by the Centers for Disease Control, more than twice as many women are shot and killed by their husbands or lovers than by strangers. Usually, it happens in the midst of an argument; he gets angry and he gets a gun. Sometimes, it's the very gun she bought to "protect" herself.

The American debate over gun control is becoming more heated. On one side, groups like the Coalition to Stop Gun Violence—an umbrella organization with chapters in Seattle and other U.S. cities—want laws that would limit the sale of high-risk handguns and assault weapons. On the other side, groups like the NRA argue that good people need those guns to protect themselves against the bad guys. It's true that, law or no law, some criminals will always manage to steal, smuggle, or somehow get their hands on guns. Today, one of their best sources is law-abiding people whose guns are lost or stolen.

The fear is real. Even in Vancouver, some people wish they were safer. Ray Eagle, who heads the city's Coalition for Gun Control, points to Great Britain and Japan, two countries where the laws are stricter, guns are fewer, and murders are rarer than in both the United States and Canada. Opponents of gun control prefer to look to Israel and Switzerland, two countries with very high rates of gun ownership and very low rates of murder. But international comparisons don't prove very much for either side; the picture is confused by the different cultures and economies.

A Cultural Difference

Opponents of gun control also like to quote from a study by Dr. Brandon Centerwall of the University of Washington. He compared the states and provinces that are neighbors along the U.S.-Canada border. Unlike the Seattle-Vancouver study, he found no connection between the number of guns and the number of homicides. Some scientists, though, feel the Centerwall study is seriously flawed, mostly because he didn't include the big cities where so much American violence takes place. To make the states and provinces more "alike," they say, he focused on the lower-risk rural areas, typical of Canada, and excluded such armed camps as Detroit and New York City from his comparison.

Americans have a firm grip on the handgun trigger. "A gun is a symbol of power. It is the great equalizer," explains Dr. Joyce Brothers. "And if you've ever watched a man play with his gun, clean it and polish it, you know that it's also a phallic symbol. That may be why they keep making guns bigger, more power-ful, more capable of shooting more bullets. It's that old school-yard game of 'mine is bigger than yours.'"

The gun carries the same symbolism in Canada, but there is a cultural difference. "We have different national myths," explains Wendy Cukier, a history professor at Ryerson Polytechnical Insti-tute in Toronto. "Your quintessential hero is the lone cowboy with his six-shooter. Ours is a figure of law, the Royal Canadian Mountie.

"Americans are passionate about individual rights and liber-ties. Canadians are more willing to restrict those rights for the common good. Your Declaration of Independence talks of 'life, liberty, and the pursuit of happiness.' Our Charter of Rights talks of 'life, liberty, and security.'"

Meanwhile, the death toll mounts on this side of the border. Guns are the least regulated, least controlled consumer product on the American market. Every two years, more Americans are killed by guns at home than were killed in all the years of the Vietnam war. In 1992, for the first time in history, more people in Texas were killed by guns than were killed by cars.

CHANGING OPINIONS

Yet something is changing. For the first time, in a recent poll, most Americans say they favor some form of gun control. They are worried about shattered lives and grieving families; and gunfire in the streets, the schools, the post offices, and fast-food restaurants.

In Vancouver, there is proof that gun-control laws can make a difference for people just like us. In Seattle, there is the voice of a grieving mother. "Someone's right to have a gun," says Joanne Wallace, "took away my right to have a son."

"Any gun-control measure that makes weapons harder to get for good guys than for bad guys ... would likely produce more violence rather than less."

PRIVATE OWNERSHIP OF HANDGUNS LEADS TO LOWER RATES OF HANDGUN VIOLENCE

Daniel D. Polsby

In the following viewpoint, Daniel D. Polsby maintains that people without access to firearms are easy prey for those who do have guns. This situation often leads to high levels of violence, he contends, as those who are armed take advantage of those who are not. Polsby argues that if most citizens are armed, society is generally more peaceable because criminals are wary of attacking someone who may have a gun. Polsby is Kirkland and Ellis Professor of Law at Northwestern University in Evanston, Illinois.

As you read, consider the following questions:

1. What examples does Polsby present to support his contention that societies in which most people are armed are safer than those in which only a few are armed?
2. According to the author, why do some heavily armed neighborhoods experience high rates of crime?
3. In Polsby's opinion, why is hiring more police officers an inadequate means of increasing security?

From Daniel D. Polsby, "Equal Protection." Reprinted, with permission, from the October 1993 issue of *Reason* magazine. Copyright 1993 by the Reason Foundation, 3415 S. Sepulveda Blvd., Suite 400, Los Angeles, CA 90034.

By the summer of 1992, what was briefly the independent republic of Bosnia-Herzegovina had been reduced to a few besieged enclaves and a seat in the United Nations. In the process, perhaps 200,000 Bosnians had been killed, and 2 million had been driven from their homes. Yet Western leaders were still dithering about whether to lift the two-year-old U.N. arms embargo that had prevented the Bosnian Muslims from effectively defending themselves since the civil war began in early 1992. . . .

AVERTING A WAR

How did the poorly armed Bosnian Muslims, the chief victims of the war, come to be surrounded by well-armed enemies? Things went quite differently in the initially lethal skirmishes between Serbs and Croats in the north. There, after some fighting, Serbia cut a deal, settling for a relatively small share of Croatia. The Croats' military power was nowhere near enough to conquer the Serbs. It was merely enough to make the Serbs appreciate the advantages of peace. Guns did not so much win a war as avert one.

The Bosnian Muslims were not so fortunate. For the most part they were unarmed, and the arms embargo left them helpless against Croat and Serb enemies who wanted their land. Margaret Thatcher, as usual among the first of the world's politicians to discern the obvious, had warned for several months that the embargo spelled disaster for the Muslim people of Bosnia. Until "ethnic cleansing" proved her point, respectable opinion was very much against her views. Throughout Europe and in the United States, it had been a bipartisan article of faith that the only hope of peace in the Balkans lay in diplomacy aided by an arms embargo. . . .

The result has been gun control, writ large: a scheme aimed at limiting violence that instead encourages predators to take whatever they want. Both the U.N. arms embargo and domestic gun control are based on the notion that the accumulation of weapons as such tends to encourage violence. The chances for peace and security can thus be enhanced by limiting or reducing the total number of weapons. . . .

THE RATE OF RETURN

Modern strategic theory rejects the weapons-violence hypothesis, focusing on stability rather than stockpiles. It starts with the proposition that people tend to pursue the course of action that they believe will give them the maximum return. Hence the likelihood of violence depends on how the expected rate of return on violence compares with the alternatives.

If you can grab an island (or a purse) that belongs to someone else with complete certainty of getting away with it at zero cost, it does not automatically follow that you will grab it. But your probability of grabbing it will be greater than if you think you have a significant chance of getting killed in the attempt—especially if you think the current owner makes the same estimate of the odds. More generally, when the expected value of attacking falls to a value equal to or less than the expected value of doing nothing, rational people will do nothing. . . .

VIOLENCE IN THE OLD WEST

Consider an example of violence that should have happened but didn't. Purdue University economist John Umbeck has investigated the formation and initial distribution of property rights in the High Sierra gold fields in the middle of the 19th century. After gold was discovered at Sutter's Mill in 1848, many thousands of prospectors poured into the hills, staked out claims, and removed minerals with a value (in today's money) in the hundreds of millions of dollars. The gold fields comprised an area of some 30,000 square miles in the California mountains. There was no civic infrastructure there at all—no towns, no highways, no lawmen, and, perhaps most significant of all, no official law for them to enforce anyway. The military governor of California had recently nullified by proclamation the Mexican land law that had previously governed the region, without proclaiming any substitute for it, temporary or permanent. Virtually all the '49ers were carrying firearms or kept them handy. Umbeck was struck by an odd fact: There was very little violence.

Another story from the old West makes a similar point. In 1889 the great Oklahoma Land Rush began. Until the late 1880s the United States respected Indian claims to Oklahoma, which meant that white people couldn't legally own land there. Through a process that no one should be proud of, this deal was busted, and a portion of Oklahoma, about 20 percent of its territory at first, was opened to settlement, beginning on a certain day at a certain hour. Oklahoma real estate was valuable stuff, just waiting to be claimed. The people who went in to settle it, like the '49ers, were mostly armed. But according to Washington College historian Robert Day, who has studied the period, they accomplished their objective essentially without violence.

These findings should surprise anyone who believes that "weapons cause violence." Not only were the Oklahomans and '49ers heavily armed, they were poor even by the hard-scrabble standards of their time. They must have been ambitious for wealth, and they probably felt that they had little to lose. From such a mix of passions and motives and guns, there ought to be one gunfight after another, as always happens in the movies—until one fierce soldier of fortune survives to grab all the gold in California, and all the farms in Oklahoma, for himself. If weapons cause violence, it's strange that things did not work out this way.

Reprinted by permission: Tribune Media Services.

Of course, not all frontier tales are of harmony and accord; sometimes armed populations did behave violently, and sometimes they still do. The important point is that sometimes they do and sometimes they don't. The fact that heavily armed people commonly do behave themselves throws down a gauntlet in front of the weapons-violence hypothesis. The theory definitely does not predict that a large, disorganized group of heavily armed men rushing headlong after the same treasure will ever behave in a consistently peaceable manner.

Umbeck offers an intriguing explanation for the low level of violence. He observes that violence is much more likely when there are large perceived differences in the ability of individuals to use force effectively. In the California gold fields and later in the Oklahoma Land Rush, everybody was about equally armed (as Umbeck notes, they didn't call the six-shooter the "equalizer" for nothing). To some extent this sort of equality is a matter of perceptions. But if perceptions tend to track underlying reality in the long run, then in the long run it is a matter of fact as well. A peaceable equilibrium, however tense, tends to prevail in a world where everyone reasonably fears retaliation from, or on behalf of, potential victims. . . .

VIOLENCE AND SOCIAL DISINTEGRATION

One sees the converse result, an equilibrium of violence and reciprocated violence, in many city neighborhoods where high levels of arms are combined with a weak social structure. Although we are accustomed to reading social disintegration from statistics that tell of high infant mortality, low graduation rates, or the bad condition of the housing stock, what is actually crucial is not that these conditions exist but that they persist, despite significant efforts to get rid of them.

It has been something of a puzzle for a generation of policy makers why, despite numerous, expensive efforts to fix them, these problems have been so hard to solve. From the viewpoint of strategic theory, however, there is no puzzle. What causes disintegration—the falling apart of things in such a way that they cannot simply be put back together—is a structure of incentives in which cooperation makes no sense.

When people do not believe that their own or anyone else's rights will be protected or wrongs rebuked, cooperation is the behavior of a sucker. In strategic terms, a disintegrated social world simulates a world of strangers. Dealings between strangers are precarious because a person cannot reasonably expect that cooperation will be reciprocated. In a world of strangers, self-interest is all on the side of selfish non-cooperation—vandalizing property, not flushing toilets after using them, cheating in transactions.

What all this suggests is that arms per se are not the issue, a conclusion that has obvious relevance to the gun-control debate. Gun-control laws usually aim to reduce the absolute number of firearms in circulation, but this is not at all important to the violence rate. What is important is the existence of a robust equilibrium between lawful and unlawful force. . . .

MORE POLICE OFFICERS ARE NOT THE ANSWER

In theory, one way of achieving such an equilibrium would be simply to hire more police officers. But in practice there is no reasonable prospect of hiring nearly enough police officers to serve as an adequate second-strike surrogate in any American city. Do the math. Each new police officer adds about $60,000 per year to a city's payroll costs. If each officer works 2,000 duty hours per year, it will cost a quarter of a million dollars just to add a single additional officer to each shift. No serious student of public administration believes it is feasible to address existing shortfalls in security services this way.

GUN CONTROL'S EFFECTS

It is always possible, however, to make a bad situation worse. Gun-control laws discourage a private alternative to hiring more police officers by making it harder for the average citizen to obtain a firearm. Indeed, gun control has a disproportionate impact on people who want firearms for legitimate reasons. Both potential victims and criminals seek guns for essentially the same purpose—to get tactical dominance in a confrontation with another person. But criminals know for certain that they'll need their guns, because they plan to have hostile interactions with other people. Law-abiding people, on the other hand, will need their guns only if confronted with a situation in which threatening to use lethal force is both legal and feasible.

AN IMPACT ON CRIMINAL BEHAVIOR

If a significant number of law-abiding people made a habit of carrying guns in public, they could create a general deterrent to crime. In *Armed and Considered Dangerous: A Survey of Felons and Their Firearms*, sociologists James D. Wright and Peter H. Rossi report that most felons worry more about encountering armed victims than about getting arrested. This fear has a real impact on criminal behavior.

Jacob Sullum, *Reason*, March 1994.

So even if the good guys and the bad guys each assign identical values to dominating a hostile encounter, bad guys will still value guns more, because on average they will be more certain of having such encounters. So there is some wisdom to the old NRA slogan, "If guns are outlawed, only outlaws will have guns." Gun control tends to put potential victims at a disadvantage relative to criminals.

This will remain true as long as guns are available in significant numbers. Whatever the obstacles to gun ownership, criminals will have a stronger incentive to overcome them. But what if guns were eliminated completely, or nearly so? A society with no guns to speak of might possibly be safer and less violent than the one in which we live. A different sort of equilibrium might prevail—the equilibrium of doves rather than the equilibrium

31

of hawks. This dream may or may not appeal to you. The crucial point is that it's not likely to be realized. It would require the government to confiscate some 200 million privately owned firearms and prevent future production or smuggling.

THE EFFECTS OF MORE FIREARMS

In the real world, security would be enhanced by encouraging the distribution of more arms rather than less. Certain categories of city dwellers have a very low statistical probability of engaging in predatory behavior. Social-security pensioners, virtually all adult females with clean criminal and psychiatric records and no history of substance abuse, and most employed men over 40 with similarly clean backgrounds are all essentially invisible in the crime statistics. Any such person who is prepared to learn what is necessary in order to handle a sidearm safely and appropriately ought to be encouraged—not merely permitted—to acquire that knowledge and carry the weapon, as police officers do, wherever they go.

Everyone appreciates that the presence of armed police officers in a neighborhood makes it a more secure place than it would be in their absence. Armed civilians of equally good character and with equivalent firearms training would be useful in a similar way, and tens of thousands of such people live and work in every big city in the country. One should think of them as auxiliary peace officers, not vigilantes, for there is no reason to believe that they would act beyond the law. Common law has always allowed self-help when regular legal remedies have been inadequate. Self-help means individuals acting under legal sanction but on their own initiative to defend important interests that court officers and police cannot protect.

Self-help is not "taking the law into your own hands." It is the law currently in every state and has been a part of the Western legal tradition practically from biblical times. Any gun-control measure that makes weapons harder to get for good guys than for bad guys certainly complicates self-help to some extent and would likely produce more violence rather than less. Lawmakers would be better advised to consider how to help people organize to defend themselves from violence that the police cannot possibly stop.

CONVENTIONAL WISDOM IS WRONG

The advice offered here runs counter to conventional wisdom, to say the least. But conventional wisdom has generally been wrong about arms policy. It predicted that keeping weapons out

of Bosnia would lead to peace. It overestimated the law's abili
to get guns away from predators and keep them away and ove
estimated the ability of the police force to protect disarme
civilians. It has made its futile pursuit of first-best solutions (tha
is, universal disarmament) the enemy of achievable second-bes
ones. It has thereby made a mess that will not get better by continuing to wish for a return to some imaginary square one
where nobody had a gun or a reason to use one.

"Studies have shown . . . that [laws
banning most handgun purchases]
significantly reduce gun-related
deaths."

PRIVATE OWNERSHIP OF HANDGUNS
SHOULD BE BANNED

Carl T. Bogus

Current handgun regulations do not prevent unstable or irresponsible people from legally purchasing guns, maintains Carl T.
Bogus in the following viewpoint. Bogus argues that even exten-
sive background checks fail to identify people who would be
likely to use handguns in a dangerous manner. The only gun-
control method that will ensure Americans' safety from firearm
violence, he asserts, is to ban handgun ownership for everyone
except law enforcement officers, military personnel, and others
who can prove a special need for a gun permit. Bogus is a visiting professor at Rutgers University School of Law in Camden,
New Jersey.

As you read, consider the following questions:

1. How much has the nation's violent crime rate increased since
   1960, according to Bogus?
2. Why did it take seven years for the Brady Bill to pass, in the
   author's opinion?
3. According to Bogus, how many Americans are shot to death
   every sixteen months?

Carl T. Bogus, "How Not to Be the NRA," Tikkun, January/February 1994. Reprinted
from TIKKUN MAGAZINE, A BI-MONTHLY JEWISH CRITIQUE OF POLITICS, CULTURE,
AND SOCIETY. Subscriptions are $31.00 per year from TIKKUN, 251 West 100th Street,
5th floor, New York, NY 10025.

Recently, I met a prominent attorney who had been shot. He was on the way to his office early one morning when he was greeted by a young woman holding a .357 magnum. He recognized her immediately; she was a former client who had discharged him after he suggested she needed psychiatric help. Now she emphasized her displeasure by pulling the trigger.

The first bullet missed, but the second hit him squarely in the chest. He thought he was dying. He was flown by helicopter to a Philadelphia hospital, where doctors discovered he was a lucky man. The bullet had grazed his heart and broke a few ribs, but he would survive.

A Violent Nation

What the lawyer learned at the hospital, however, surprised him almost as much as looking down the barrel of a gun. Hospital emergency rooms today resemble MASH units. In the course of a year, police cruisers, ambulances, helicopters, and just plain wobbly legs carry more than 600 gunshot victims into the hospital in which the lawyer found himself—one of many local hospitals that routinely treat gunshot victims. And Philadelphia is not an especially violent city; its violent crime rate is only half that of Boston, Dallas, Los Angeles, New York, or even Kansas City, Missouri, and less than a third that of Atlanta, Miami, or Newark, New Jersey.

Yet Philadelphia is far more dangerous today than ever before. In 1960, the violent crime rate in Philadelphia was 336 per 100,000 residents; by 1991, it had skyrocketed to 1,429 per 100,000. And Philadelphia is typical; in the nation as a whole, the violent crime rate has more than quadrupled since 1960.

As the lawyer with a hole near his heart lay recovering in the hospital, facts like these were called to his attention by his physicians, who were understandably frustrated and angry over the increasing carnage with which they must deal. The lawyer had something of a near-death-bed conversion experience; he decided he must help bring gun control to America. And he knew just how to go about it: He would use his skills as a mediator to bring together gun control advocates and the NRA [National Rifle Association]. He would help them find a middle ground on which they could agree, help them jointly to fashion a "sensible" gun control proposal. It was a task not unlike others he had undertaken in his professional career—helping two seemingly intractable parties recognize that a compromise was possible.

The lawyer may be forgiven for his naiveté. After all, nearly everyone labors under two misconceptions. The first is that the

NRA singlehandedly blocks the path to gun control in the United States. The second is that the NRA represents the views of hunters and sportsmen, who have not yet awakened to the rising tide of violence. If these views were accurate, it would be reasonable to try to fashion a deal that both provided for effective gun control and assured sportsmen that they were not starting down a slippery slope that would end with the government confiscating hunting rifles. But as one can learn from *NRA: Money, Firepower, and Fear* by Josh Sugarmann or *Under Fire: The NRA and the Battle for Gun Control* by Osha Gray Davidson, these are, at best, half-truths. The key to achieving effective gun control lies not in converting its opponents, or in finding middle ground, but in galvanizing its supporters.

MAKE HANDGUN POSSESSION ILLEGAL

The more cerebral defenders of gun ownership are wont to say, "We don't need any more gun-control laws. There are plenty of such laws on the books now." But they neglect to point out that all these laws are "after the fact" laws: greater punishment for a crime committed with a gun and a fine or occasionally more serious punishment for a person "caught" with a gun without a permit. We're willing to disarm gun wielders only *after* they have killed, maimed, or used their guns to terrorize innocent people. What crap! . . .

We [should] make handgun possession illegal, with or without a permit, except for law enforcement and other authorized personnel, and follow up by insisting that our various governments appropriate sufficient funds to buy back the then-outlawed handguns for the purpose of destroying them. It would be money well spent.

Robert E. Burns, *U.S. Catholic*, January 1994.

This is not to deny that the NRA is large or politically powerful. Due to a vigorous campaign following the L.A. riots in 1992, NRA membership may be higher today than ever before, slightly exceeding three million. But while an organization of this size is large, it is not unique. The American Legion and Mothers Against Drunk Driving each have slightly more than three million members, for example, and the American Association of Retired Persons (AARP) has 33 million. While the two national groups devoted solely to advocating gun control are relatively small when compared to the NRA—Handgun Control, Inc. (HCI) has about 300,000 members and the Coalition Against Gun Violence about 75,000—a host of other politically potent organizations also strongly support gun control—including the American Bar Association, American Medical Association, National Education Association, AARP, AFL-CIO, American Federation of State, County and Municipal Employees, the Fraternal Order of Police, and virtually every other national police organization, and religious groups of all denominations—from the American Jewish Committee to the National Council of Churches to the Mennonite Central Committee.

The power of the NRA purse is also overrated. The NRA's PAC [political action committee] disbursed $5.7 million during the 1991–92 election cycle, making it the fourth biggest spending PAC in the nation. This dwarfs Handgun Control's PAC, which spent $380,000 during the same period, yet it represents only a tiny fraction of the nearly $400 million spent by all PACs during that time. Even $5.7 million is not a lot of money when it is spread not only among federal candidates but in state races throughout the country.

Support for Gun Control

Ultimately what counts is not members or money but votes, and no asset is more important than public opinion. Here there is no contest: The public overwhelmingly supports gun control. Sixty-eight percent favor banning cheap handguns known as "Saturday Night Specials," 72 percent favor banning semi-automatic assault weapons, 78 percent want laws relating to the sale of firearms to be more strict, 80 percent favor handgun registration and 95 percent favor a seven-day waiting period for handgun purchases. The near consensus of opinion makes it difficult to describe these as "controversial" issues.

The single question on which the public is truly split is whether there ought to be a total ban on handguns. But the percentage of Americans who would support a total handgun ban has been climbing.

Strikingly, according to the polls, the views of gun owners are virtually identical with those of the public-at-large. "The hardline views of the NRA are crafted not from the majority of gun owners, or even from its members, but from its leadership and an activist core of 600,000 members," Sugarmann writes. This group—which zealously opposes any form of firearm regulation—controls the internal politics of the NRA. No group of this size, however, has the power to frustrate the national will.

Why, then, have gun control efforts been unsuccessful?

It is not because gun control forces have overreached. In 1986, Handgun Control, Inc. decided to devote itself to passing

37

the Brady bill, which would establish a national seven-day waiting period for handgun purchases. Its strategy was simple: This was so modest a measure that any opposition would appear unreasonable. As someone succinctly put it, anyone who can't wait a week to get a handgun is exactly the kind of person who shouldn't have one.

HCI had an appealing way to market the Brady bill. Leading the fight would be Sarah Brady, wife of Jim Brady, President Reagan's press secretary who had been shot in the head during John Hinckley's assassination attempt on Ronald Reagan. Sarah would be able to begin every speech by saying, "I am a Republican and a conservative," and preach simple common sense.

About half the states already had handgun waiting periods, some up to fifteen days. A 1981 Gallup Poll had found that 91 percent of the public favored a twenty-one-day waiting period for handgun purchases. Wanting to appear moderate, however, HCI sought only a seven-day waiting period. Its immediate objective was not effective gun control legislation but a political victory.

Founded in 1974, HCI had been unsuccessful throughout its organizational life. Not only had it failed at getting any new gun control laws enacted, it also was unable to protect existing federal legislation. In 1985, the NRA succeeded in having Congress pass the McClure-Volkmer Act, gutting key provisions of the Gun Control Act of 1968, which had been enacted after the assassinations of Martin Luther King and Robert Kennedy. Although HCI would not admit this publicly, federal gun laws are more feeble today than they were before the organization was established.

There is superficial sense to a strategy premised on the theory that the way to prevail in the future is to be perceived as having beaten the NRA in the past. The reasoning runs as follows: The NRA's principal asset is its image of omnipotence and invincibility. Legislators believe the NRA has the power to deny them re-election (NRA omnipotence), and that it is pointless to take risks or expend political capital on the issue because gun control legislation won't pass anyway (NRA invincibility). Thus it is crucial to win a battle—any battle—to destroy the NRA mystique and free legislators to do the right thing.

FLAWED REASONING

But the reasoning, and thus the strategy, are flawed. By choosing to make the Brady bill its flagship proposal, HCI signaled that it did not believe it could win a meaningful victory. What HCI considered the strength of the proposal—its moderateness—

was also its weakness. HCI did not so much look reasonable as afraid. The Brady bill was simply too weak to become a priority issue for voters. Few believed it would have any appreciable effect on gun violence. While it seemed like a nice idea (good enough for voters, when asked, to tell pollsters they favored it), it wasn't something voters thought would make a difference. Ross Perot expressed this view during one of the 1992 presidential debates when he said the Brady bill was a "timid step in the right direction but it won't fix [the problem], so why pass a law that won't fix it?" Thus a bill that was supposed to be politically irresistible failed for seven years.

A SAFE NATION HAS NO GUNS

Those nations that tightly restrict gun ownership are nations where, generally, children can still play outside, adults can stroll at night and families can picnic in parks without fear. They are nations where private security guards are not yet ubiquitous, as they are in the United States. And they are nations where people usually go about their daily lives free of the shadow of drive-by shootings, mass murder-suicides and domestic quarrels that escalate into homicide. The direction for the United States is also clear: We must enact gun-control laws that work better than current ones. We must do so soon and we must do so nationally. What's required is a near-total ban on the manufacture, sale and possession of handguns and assault weapons, leaving those weapons in the hands of law enforcement officials alone. Individuals should be permitted to own sport guns and rifles only if they have submitted to a background check and passed a course in safe weapons use.

Los Angeles Times, November 8, 1993.

Now that the Brady bill has passed, will it achieve its original objective or will it be a Pyrrhic victory?

It has taken so long to achieve so little that neither the Clinton administration nor the congressional leadership are likely to be eager for another handgun proposal. Nevertheless, public alarm over rising violence may force gun control onto the national agenda. One of the unfortunate legacies of the Brady bill, however, is that it conditioned opinion leaders to accept a flawed premise about how gun control must work.

TWO APPROACHES

There are only two basic approaches to controlling handguns: either (1) everyone may have a handgun except those who fall into a prohibited category; or (2) no one may have a handgun except those who fall into a permitted category. We can call the first a general eligibility system and the second a restrictive permitting system. The difference between the two is profound. The Brady bill is grounded in the first system, but only the second offers a genuine prospect of reducing gun violence.

To appreciate the difference, consider the case most often associated with the Brady bill—the shooting of Jim Brady. John Hinckley purchased his handgun from a Dallas pawnshop five months before his assassination attempt on Reagan. Sarah Brady argues, nevertheless, that a waiting period would have stopped this sale because it would have given the police time to check Hinckley out—to see whether he was a minor, a convicted felon, mentally unstable, or otherwise prohibited from owning a handgun.

Hinckley, of course, was mentally unstable, but would the police have discovered this? Probably not. About two million handguns are sold every year in the United States, and it is impossible for the police to investigate every purchaser. They might check handgun applications against felony records, but neither Hinckley nor 71 percent of the people who commit handgun murders are previously convicted felons. Sarah Brady argues that the police would have stopped the Hinckley sale because he was not living at the locale he listed as his home address. Yet there was nothing that would have prompted the police to discover this; Hinckley presented a valid Texas driver's license listing the address at which he had lived when he was a student in Texas.

A general eligibility system cannot work. There is no feasible way to identify people with criminal intentions, violent propensities, psychoses, uncontrollable tempers, suicidal depressions, or those who become dangerous when drunk or are irresponsible enough to leave a loaded gun where a child may find it. Moreover, even if all this were possible, the general eligibility system would still fail because all someone who cannot buy a handgun need do is have someone buy it for him.

THE RESTRICTIVE PERMITTING SYSTEM

Studies have shown, however, that restrictive permitting systems significantly reduce gun-related deaths. When the District of Columbia adopted a restrictive permitting system in 1976, for example, gun-related murders and suicides were both cut by about one-quarter while there was no corresponding change in the immediately surrounding areas of Maryland and Virginia. This law did not turn Washington into the Garden of Eden, of course, yet it had a marked effect even though it was implemented on a small political island.

Canada, which uses a restrictive permitting system, offers another basis for comparison. Epidemiologists studied crime in Seattle and Vancouver, two cities with remarkably similar geographies, histories, population sizes, demographics, cultures, and overall crime rates. The burglary rates were nearly identical in both cities, for example, as were rates of assault and murder with knives and clubs. But the risk of being shot to death was nearly five times higher in Seattle, and the chance of being assaulted at gunpoint in Seattle was eight times greater than in Vancouver.

Under a restrictive permitting system, only certain categories of people may own handguns—law enforcement officers, military personnel, licensed security guards, and persons who can demonstrate to the satisfaction of the police or a court that they have a special need for one. A "special need" must be more than a generalized desire for self-defense; there must be a concrete reason to fear attack. Indeed, as confirmed in a study published in 1993 in *The New England Journal of Medicine*, a gun in the home actually increases the risk that the owner or a family member will be shot.

The restrictive permitting system is based on the concept that the police can best assess both someone's need for a handgun and his or her trustworthiness. Someone facing a genuine emergency is better off under a system in which he or she can go to the police station and explain the situation in person; and the police are better able to evaluate such a request when the applicant is in front of them.

The police should have discretion to tailor permits to particular circumstances and to grant permits on the spot when necessary. Permits would be issued for specified periods and for particular guns, which must have engraved serial numbers and be presented for inspection. Rejected applicants would have a right to judicial review. Under a restrictive permitting system, two million people would not be able to buy handguns every year—and that is precisely the point.

BETTER THAN THE ALTERNATIVES

Opponents will argue that such a system will not be perfect. They will be right, but no system can be perfect. The issue is not whether a restrictive permitting system will be perfect but whether it will be better than alternatives. Colin Ferguson sat out California's fifteen-day waiting period before buying the 9-

millimeter Ruger he used to shoot twenty-three people on the Long Island Railroad in December 1993. Lee Harvey Oswald would have had no trouble passing a shooting skills course, which may be the next step down the dead-end street of a general eligibility system. Milquetoast measures will not do when more Americans are being shot to death in the United States every sixteen months than were killed in combat during the entire Vietnam War.

If a restrictive permitting system sounds extreme, it is in part because for so long the gun control debate has been framed by the Brady bill. Yet it is the medicine America needs.

"Because guns empower the weak
against the strong, and because
victims are generally weaker than
felons, widespread gun ownership is
a net benefit for society."

PRIVATE OWNERSHIP OF HANDGUNS SHOULD BE ENCOURAGED

Don B. Kates Jr.

In the following viewpoint, Don B. Kates Jr. argues that laws that prevent law-abiding citizens from owning guns benefit criminals instead of the general public. Rather than reducing crime, he contends, bans on gun ownership make criminals feel safer because they know that their potential victims are unarmed and less able to defend themselves. Studies show that citizens who are armed, or who are thought to be armed, are less likely to be victimized, Kates maintains. Kates is a civil-liberties lawyer, criminologist, and editor of Firearms and Violence.

As you read, consider the following questions:

1. According to Kates, what three research findings did Gary Kleck report in his book Point Blank: Guns and Violence in America?
2. What is responsible for much criminal activity, according to Ted Robert Gurr, as cited by Kates?
3. According to the author, what percentage of felons in a National Institute of Justice survey said that they were deterred from their crime because their victim was armed?

Don B. Kates Jr., "Shot Down," National Review, March 6, 1995. Copyright ©1995 by National Review, Inc., 150 E. 35th St., New York, NY 10016.

Criminologists, criminals, and cops all have a professional interest in crime. It is therefore significant that criminological research has generally validated the skepticism of both police and criminals about the effectiveness of gun control. Yet the consensus among these three sets of professionals has received little attention in the popular media.

Surprisingly, in light of the fervent support for stringent gun control that many academics expressed in the 1960s, serious research in this area did not begin until the 1970s. That research demonstrates that no amount of control over mere weaponry can overcome the fundamental socio-cultural and economic determinants of crime. Indeed, the evidence indicates that banning gun possession by the general public is actually counterproductive.

ARGUMENTS AGAINST GUN CONTROL

The most prolific researcher in this area is Gary Kleck of Florida State University's School of Criminology. His encyclopedic 1991 book, *Point Blank: Guns and Violence in America*, has won high praise even from academics distressed by its findings. Broadly speaking, those findings are: 1) Gun possession by ordinary citizens is not a problem; the perpetrators of gun crime and accidents are aberrant individuals with histories of substance abuse, violence, felonies, and other dangerous behavior. 2) While outlawing possession of guns by such people is plainly sensible, it can bring at best marginal benefit as long as the fundamental determinants of their behavior remain unchanged. 3) Because guns empower the weak against the strong, and because victims are generally weaker than felons, widespread gun ownership is a net benefit for society.

Based on surveys of both the general populace and incarcerated felons, Kleck finds that gun-armed victims rout criminals three to four times more often than gun-armed criminals attack victims. And a victim who resists with a gun is only half as likely to be injured as a victim who submits—and far less likely to be robbed or raped.

In 1993 the American Society of Criminology declared Kleck's book the single most important contribution to criminological research in the previous three years. Kleck's findings are so unimpeachable that critics often resort to ad hominem attacks. They falsely accuse Kleck of being a National Rifle Association member, minion, or even employee. In fact, Kleck, a liberal Democrat and opponent of the death penalty, is a member not of the NRA but of Amnesty International and the American Civil Liberties Union (ACLU). Moreover, Kleck started out on the other side of the gun-control debate. In a 1991 speech to the National Academy of Sciences, he said:

> When I began my research on guns in 1976, like most academics, I was a believer in the "anti-gun" thesis. . . . It seemed then like self-evident common sense which hardly needed to be empirically tested. . . . [But] the best currently available evidence, imperfect though it is (and must always be), indicates that general gun availability has no measurable net positive effect on rates of homicide, suicide, robbery, assault, rape, or burglary in the U.S. . . . Further, when victims have guns, it is less likely aggressors will attack or injure them and less likely they will lose property in a robbery. . . . The positive associations often found between aggregate levels of violence and gun ownership appear to be primarily due to violence increasing gun ownership, rather than the reverse.

Other scholars have also changed their views. University of Maryland political scientist Ted Robert Gurr and State University of New York criminologist Hans Toch were closely associated with the Eisenhower Commission, which concluded in the Sixties that "reducing the availability of the handgun will reduce firearms violence." Based on subsequent research, however, each now repudiates this judgment. "When used for protection," Toch writes, "firearms can seriously inhibit aggression and can provide a psychological buffer against the fear of crime. Furthermore, the fact that national patterns show little violent crime where guns are most dense implies that guns do not elicit aggression in any meaningful way. Quite the contrary, these findings suggest that high saturations of guns in places, or something correlated with that condition, inhibit illegal aggression."

Gurr has come to believe that handgun prohibition "would criminalize much of the citizenry but have only marginal effects on criminals," while "overemphasis on such proposals diverts attention from the kinds of conditions that are responsible for much of our crime, such as persisting poverty for the black underclass and some whites and Hispanics." Gurr adds that "guns can be an effective defense," noting that UCLA historian Roger McGrath's evidence from the 19th-century American West "shows that widespread gun ownership deterred" acquisitive crimes. "Modern studies," he writes, "also show that widespread gun ownership deters crime. . . . Convicted robbers and burglars report that they are deterred when they think their potential targets are armed."

Indeed, felons have consistently said that banning handguns would make their lives safer and easier by disarming victims without affecting their own ability to obtain weapons. "Ban guns," said a typical convict interviewed by New York University criminologist Ernest van den Haag in the mid 1970s. "I'd love it. I'm an armed robber."

KEEPING AMERICA SAFE

When private citizens are actually permitted to do something about their own safety—patrolling shopping mall parking lots or driving hookers, pimps, and dope dealers from street corners—the more sensitive, gentle souls among us issue forth with platitudes about race and class oppression. But such action is our only real hope of returning the streets and neighborhoods of urban (and if things get worse, rural) America to law-abiding citizens.

Our federal republic will not long survive national gun control legislation meant to disarm good citizens. . . . Presently, such legislation threatens the original American federal system by preventing the states and their county subdivisions from defending themselves against the tyranny of street crime or of "consolidated" government.

Michael Hill, Chronicles, March 1995.

In 1982 the Chicago suburb of Morton Grove received nationwide publicity for enacting the nation's first handgun ban. Surprisingly little attention was paid to two remarkable responses. One was a letter an inmate in a Florida prison wrote the editor of a local newspaper: "If guns are banned, then I as a criminal feel a lot safer. When a thief breaks into someone's house or property, the first thing to worry about is getting shot by the owner. But now, it seems we won't have to worry about that anymore." Branding it a "fantasy that just because guns are outlawed we, the crooks, can't get guns," the author asserted that "the only people who can't are the ones we victimize. . . . Drugs are against the law. Does that stop us? It's also against the law to rob and steal. But does a law stop us? One more thing: I thank you, the public, for giving me this fine opportunity to further my criminal career."

Similarly, the editor of the inmate newspaper at the Illinois Correctional Center in Menard "made it a point to get the views of those in the real know—convicts here for armed robbery, some of them extremely professional individuals with years of experience in their chosen field. The[y] . . . were unanimous that you in Morton Grove are making things a bit easier for us. . . . [The] law is meaningless and useless in curbing crime.

However, it is very effective in curbing the general populace. This coming from 'hardened criminals,' professionals, convicts . . . someone should listen!"

Perhaps the National Institute of Justice did listen. In 1983 it funded a survey of two thousand felons in state prisons across the U.S. In addition to overwhelmingly endorsing the views set out above, 39 per cent of the felons in the NIJ survey said they had aborted at least one crime because they believed the intended victim was armed; 8 per cent had done so "many" times; 34 per cent had been "scared off, shot at, wounded, or captured by an armed victim"; and 69 per cent knew at least one acquaintance who had had such an experience.

Thirty-four per cent of the felons said that in contemplating a crime they either "often" or "regularly" worried that they "might get shot at by the victim." Asked about criminals in general, 56 per cent of the inmates agreed that "a criminal is not going to mess around with a victim he knows is armed with a gun"; 57 per cent agreed that "most criminals are more worried about meeting an armed victim than they are about running into the police"; 58 per cent agreed that "a store owner who is known to keep a gun on the premises is not going to get robbed very often"; and 74 per cent agreed that "one reason burglars avoid houses when people are home is that they fear being shot during the crime."

GUN CONTROL IS NOT THE ANSWER

Since 1976 the District of Columbia has had the country's most extreme gun law: no civilian may buy or carry a handgun, nor may any gun be kept loaded or assembled in a home for self-defense. Nevertheless, Washington has one of the highest homicide rates in the country. In 1992 *Washington Post* reporters interviewed the 114 inmates in D.C.'s Lorton Prison who had been convicted of at least one gun crime. The consensus was clear: "Gun control is not the answer, the inmates agreed." And they anticipated no difficulty obtaining an illegal gun. Though many claimed to want to go straight, 25 per cent flatly said they would get a gun as soon as they emerged from prison.

A week later a newspaper in Syracuse found similar opinions when it combined a survey of inmates in a nearby maximum-security prison with a survey of police officers in the local department. The two groups concurred that tougher gun laws would have no effect on crime; neither would banning assault weapons.

This congruence of opinion contradicts the impression that several prominent police chiefs have created that cops generally oppose civilian gun ownership. The truth is that these police chiefs were appointed precisely because their views sharply diverged from their peers'. Furthermore, strong political pressure tends to silence police administrators who oppose gun bans. In the mid 1980s Maurice Turner became Washington, D.C.'s first black police chief. When reporters inquired into the new chief's opinion of D.C.'s severe gun law, he replied that it was not just useless but actually promoted crime, since felons knew it had rendered victims defenseless. When his remarks were reported, he was called on the carpet by Mayor Marion Barry, who told him banning guns was a city policy that he was forbidden to criticize. Thereafter Chief Turner refused to comment on gun control (until he retired, whereupon he reiterated his previous views).

COULD MORE GUNS MAKE OUR STREETS SAFER?

Handgun Control, Inc. warns that "more guns lead to more deaths and injuries from gunshots." Not in Florida, they don't. More than 100,000 people have licenses to carry concealed handguns, but the abuses have been rare. By the end of 1993, only 17 licenses had been revoked because the licensee committed a crime with a firearm. . . .

Permit holders could eventually deter crime, as crooks begin to perceive a heightened risk in their profession. The presence of guns in the home is a major reason why the high-crime United States has a lower burglary rate than England, where guns are largely forbidden and intruders don't have to worry about death from Sudden Perforation Syndrome. For those who worry that America will come to resemble the Wild West, the Independence Institute says we should be so lucky: Homicide was almost unknown in Dodge City and other gun-heavy places.

Stephen Chapman, *Conservative Chronicle*, February 8, 1995.

Boston Police Chief Robert DiGrazia, on the other hand, did sincerely champion the banning and confiscation of handguns. In 1976 he had his research division poll police opinion nationwide, hoping the results would support a Massachusetts ballot initiative to ban handguns. Thinking patrol officers would oppose the initiative, he limited the poll to administrators. Yet the survey found "a substantial majority of the respondents looked favorably on the general possession of handguns by the citizenry (excludes those with criminal records [or] history of mental instability). Strong approval was also elicited from the police administrators concerning possession of handguns in the home or place of business." The poll confirmed Chief DiGrazia's views in only one respect: the administrators agreed that officers who dealt with crime on the streets would be even more opposed to banning handguns.

A HANDGUN FOR EVERY ADULT

This pattern has been confirmed by subsequent polling. For instance, in *Law Enforcement Technology* magazine's 1991 poll of two thousand cops across the nation, 76 per cent of street officers believed that licenses to carry concealed handguns for protection should be issued to every trained, responsible adult applicant; only 59 per cent of managers agreed. Ninety-one per cent of street officers opposed banning semi-automatic "assault rifles," compared to 66 per cent of top management. On the other hand, 94 per cent of street officers felt that private citizens should keep handguns in their homes and offices for self-defense, and 93 per cent of top management agreed. Over all, 93 per cent of the respondents supported defensive ownership of handguns, 85 per cent felt gun control had little potential to reduce crime, 79 per cent opposed banning "assault weapons," and 63 per cent supported widespread carrying of concealed handguns by trained civilians.

Every year since 1988, the National Association of Chiefs of Police has polled the nation's more than fifteen thousand police agencies, with a response rate of 10 per cent or more. The respondents have consistently said that their departments are understaffed and unable to adequately protect individuals; that law-abiding, responsible adults should have the right to own "any type of firearm" for self-defense; and that banning guns will not reduce crime. In these and other surveys police generally support moderate controls, such as background checks, designed to exclude felons from gun ownership to the extent possible without obstructing defensive ownership by law-abiding citizens.

It's possible, of course, that the cops, the criminals, and the criminologists are mistaken about gun control. But given the remarkable consensus, it's time to reconsider the casual assumption that weapons cause crime.

"By the year 2000 firearms will likely supplant automobiles as the leading cause of product-related death throughout the United States."

PRIVATE OWNERSHIP OF HANDGUNS IS A PUBLIC-HEALTH HAZARD

Josh Sugarmann

In the following viewpoint, Josh Sugarmann argues that handguns are a deadly consumer product whose violent and economic toll on Americans is staggering. The costs of hospitalization, lost wages, and rehabilitation make gun violence a public-health issue, he maintains. Guns, like other potentially dangerous products, should be regulated by government agencies, Sugarmann contends. Sugarmann is the executive director of the Violence Policy Center, an educational foundation that researches firearms violence and advocates gun control. He is also the author of *NRA: Money, Firepower, and Fear*.

As you read, consider the following questions:

1. How many Americans were killed by guns in 1990, according to Sugarmann?
2. What was the lifetime economic cost of gun violence in 1985, according to the Centers for Disease Control, as cited by the author?
3. In Sugarmann's opinion, what would result if the Bureau of Alcohol, Tobacco, and Firearms regulated the design, manufacture, and sale of firearms?

Josh Sugarmann, "Reverse Fire," *Mother Jones*, January/February 1994. Reprinted with permission from *Mother Jones* magazine, ©1994, Foundation for National Progress.

For seven years gun-control advocates have lobbied for the Brady Bill, which mandates a national waiting period for buying handguns. But ironically, the bill's passage may actually benefit the gun industry. Oversold by its supporters, the Brady Bill has become synonymous in American minds with gun control itself. If violence continues once a national waiting period goes into effect (as it likely will), the gun lobby will offer the Brady Bill as proof that gun control doesn't work.

A LACK OF REGULATION

With its passage in 1993, gun-control advocates find themselves at a crossroads. We can continue to push legislation of dubious effectiveness. Or we can acknowledge that gun violence is a public-health crisis fueled by an inherently dangerous consumer product. To end the crisis, we have to regulate—or, in the case of handguns and assault weapons, completely ban—the product.

The romantic myths attached to gun ownership stop many people from thinking of them as a consumer product. As a result, the standard risk analysis applied to other potentially dangerous products—pesticides, prescription drugs, or toasters—has never been applied to firearms.

Yet guns are manufactured by corporations—with boards of directors, marketing plans, employees, and a bottom line—just like companies that manufacture toasters. What separates the gun industry from other manufacturers is lack of regulation.

For example, when a glut in the market caused handgun production to plummet from 2.6 million in 1982 to 1.4 million in 1986, the industry retooled its product line. To stimulate sales, manufacturers added firepower, technology, and capacity to their new models. The result: assault weapons, a switch from six-shot revolvers to high-capacity pistols, and increased use of plastics and high-tech additions like integral laser sights.

The industry was free to make these changes (most of which made the guns more dangerous) because guns that are 50 caliber or less and not fully automatic can be manufactured with virtually no restrictions. The Bureau of Alcohol, Tobacco, and Firearms (ATF) lacks even the common regulatory powers—including safety-standard setting and recall—granted government agencies such as the Consumer Product Safety Commission, the Food and Drug Administration, and the Environmental Protection Agency.

A DEADLY PRODUCT

Yet guns are the second most deadly consumer product (after cars) on the market. In Texas and Louisiana the firearms-related death rate already exceeds that for motor vehicles, and by the year 2000 firearms will likely supplant automobiles as the leading cause of product-related death throughout the United States.

But since Americans view firearm suicides, murders, and fatal accidents as separate problems, the enormity of America's gun crisis goes unrecognized. In 1990, American guns claimed an estimated 37,000 lives. Federal Bureau of Investigation data shows that gun murders that year reached an all-time high of 15,377; a record 12,489 involved handguns.

THE HUMAN TOLL

In 1990 (the most recent year for which statistics are available), 18,885 Americans took their own lives with firearms, and an estimated 13,030 of those deaths involved handguns. Unlike pills, gas, or razor blades—which are of limited effectiveness— guns are rarely forgiving. For example, self-inflicted cutting wounds account for 15 percent of all suicide attempts but only 1 percent of all successful suicides. Poisons and drugs account for 70 percent of suicide attempts but less than 12 percent of all suicides. Conversely, nonfatal, self-inflicted gunshot wounds are rare—yet three-fifths of all U.S. suicides involve firearms.

SURGEON GENERAL'S WARNING

Homicide, often involving guns, is a disease that is the leading cause of death for young black men, and the second-leading cause of death for all people aged fifteen to twenty-four. That *makes* it the leading health issue, particularly when guns are used in combination with drugs and alcohol. And the statistics show that is most often the case. Guns kill more teenagers than the other big killers—heart disease, cancer, and AIDS—combined.

Joycelyn Elders, *Mother Jones*, January/February 1994.

In addition to the human toll, the economic costs of not regulating guns are staggering. The Centers for Disease Control (CDC) estimated that the lifetime economic cost—hospitalization, rehabilitation, and lost wages—of firearms violence was $14.4 billion in 1985, making it the third most expensive injury category. The average lifetime cost per person for each firearms fatality—$373,520—was the highest of any injury.

Such human and economic costs are not tolerated for any other product. Many consumer products from lawn darts to the Dalkon Shield have been banned in the United States, even though they claimed only a fraction of the lives guns do in a day. The firearms industry is long overdue for the simple, regulatory oversight applied to other consumer products. For public safety, the ATF must be given authority to control the design, manufacture, distribution, and sale of firearms and ammunition.

Under such a plan, the ATF would subject each category of firearm and ammunition to an unreasonable-risk analysis to weed out products whose potential for harm outweighs any possible benefit. This would result in an immediate ban on the future production and sale of handguns and assault weapons because of their high risk and low utility.

Because they are easily concealed and accessed, handguns hold the dubious honor of being our number-one murder and suicide tool. Assault weapons—high-capacity, semiautomatic firearms designed primarily for the military and police—pose a public-safety risk as the result of their firepower. A 1989 study of ATF data conducted by Cox Newspapers found that assault firearms were twenty times more likely to turn up in crime traces than conventional firearms.

In addition, a regulatory approach to firearms would exert far greater control over the industry and its distribution network. It would not, however, affect the availability of standard sporting rifles and shotguns, which would continue to be sold because of their usefulness and relatively low risk.

A PUBLIC-HEALTH ISSUE

Such an approach is the industry's worst nightmare—conjuring images of an all-powerful "gun czar." And in a sense, gun manufacturers would be right: the ATF would become a gun czar in the same way that the EPA is a pesticide czar, the FDA is a prescription-drug-and-medical-device czar, and the Consumer Product Safety Commission is a toaster czar. Yet it is just such a regulatory approach that has dramatically reduced motor-vehicle deaths and injuries over the past twenty years.

Gun-control advocates cannot afford to spend another seven years battling over piecemeal measures that have little more to offer than good intentions. We are far past the point where registration, licensing, safety training, background checks, or waiting periods will have much effect on firearms violence. Tired of being shot and threatened, Americans are showing a deeper understanding of gun violence as a public-health issue, and are becoming aware of the need to restrict specific categories of weapons.

As America's health-care debate continues, discussion of the role of guns—from the human price paid in mortality to the dollars-and-cents cost of uninsured gunshot victims—can only help clarify that gun violence is not a crime issue but a public-health issue. This shift in attitude is apparent in the firearms component of Bill Clinton's domestic violence prevention group, which is co-chaired not only by a representative from the Justice Department—as expected—but also by a CDC official.

Even if the only legacy of this current wave of revulsion is that gun violence will now be viewed as a public-health issue, America will still have taken a very large first step toward gun sanity.

| "Far more Americans still die each year from pneumonia and influenza than perish in all—not just gun related—homicides and suicides combined."

PRIVATE OWNERSHIP OF HANDGUNS IS NOT A PUBLIC-HEALTH HAZARD

Tucker Carlson

Many doctors claim that the rate of gun violence in the United States constitutes an epidemic that can only be solved by eliminating handguns. In the following viewpoint, Tucker Carlson argues against treating handgun ownership as a public-health hazard. He claims that doctors misinterpret data to support their views that handguns are dangerous to the public. In no way can guns and gun violence be classified as a medical disease, Carlson contends. The debate over handgun violence should be left to the experts, he maintains, and not to doctors. Carlson is a staff writer for the *Weekly Standard*.

As you read, consider the following questions:
1. Why is comparing guns to pathogens inaccurate, according to Carlson?
2. What evidence does Carlson present to show that the most commonly quoted statistic of the gun-control movement is not exactly true?
3. In the author's opinion, why do people listen to doctors' opinions on gun control?

Tucker Carlson, "Handgun Control, M.D.," *Weekly Standard*, April 15, 1996. Reprinted by permission of the *Weekly Standard*.

The people chanting slogans in front of the Health and Human Services building in Washington one morning in March 1996 looked mostly like standard-issue left-wing demonstrators—angry-faced women wearing backpacks and big earrings, slope-shouldered men with ponytails and workers-of-the-world boots—in a sea of protest signs and class resentment. Yet one aspect of their appearance seemed amiss: Nearly every person present was wearing a lab coat and stethoscope. As it turned out, these weren't your ordinary peaceniks, but doctors. They had gathered to lobby for the latest addition to America's ever-expanding definition of health care: gun control.

HANDGUNS AS A DISEASE

"We don't have to have one American die from bullets," an emergency-room physician from the Midwest shouted to the crowd. "Every one of these deaths is preventable." And who will prevent them? Doctors, of course. According to a new theory gaining currency in America's medical establishment, deaths caused by firearms can no longer be classified simply as crimes or accidents. Instead, they are symptoms of illness—or, as one physician solemnly told his colleagues, of "a chronic and recurrent disease." That disease is violence. The germs that cause it are guns, especially handguns.

By the time the rally ended, the doctors seemed in high spirits, and it's no wonder. Framed in medical terms, gun-related mayhem begins to look like one of society's most easily solved problems—nothing at all like the complex affliction that has stymied the best efforts of police, judges, and criminologists for better than a century. If violence is a disease, and guns the pathogen, then the cure is simple: Get rid of the guns. Which is just what the doctors at the rally were ordering. Why didn't somebody think of this before? It worked with smallpox.

Indeed, the extinction of the smallpox virus is what many physicians have in mind when they talk about the "epidemic" of shootings sweeping the land like a plague. In the last couple of years, hospitals and doctors' groups—from the American Medical Association to the federal Centers for Disease Control and Prevention—have conducted research and formulated policies on firearms in the belief that science can conquer gun violence as surely as it once did polio. "Guns are a virus that must be eradicated," a Chicago pediatrician named Katherine Christoffel told the American Medical Association. "Get rid of the cigarettes, get rid of the secondhand smoke, and you get rid of lung disease. It's the same with guns. Get rid of the guns, get rid of the bullets, and you get rid of the deaths."

Christoffel, a one-time leader in the Radcliffe chapter of Students for a Democratic Society, has been a particularly visible proponent of the guns-as-germs theory, appearing frequently as a spokeswoman for the 50,000-member American Academy of Pediatrics, which advocates a ban on the "manufacture, sale and private possession of handguns" (and of "deadly air guns"). "Imagine that there was a new virus that suddenly was causing a dramatic rise in death," Christoffel explained to the *Chicago Tribune*. Handgun violence "is exactly the same thing. The problem is that since it involves a gun, it's easy to miss that fact. Still, this is a killer virus."

PROBLEMATIC REASONING

Talk of Ebola-like scourges makes for terrific soundbites, but this line of reasoning is a problematic guide to public policy. For one thing, guns *aren't* pathogens; not biologically, not even metaphorically. Genuine pathogens, as any doctor knows, cause disease when introduced into a pathogen-free environment. Considering that there are more than 200 million privately owned firearms in the United States, only a minuscule fraction of which are ever used in acts of violence, guns don't qualify under this definition.

Nor can gun violence, as Christoffel and others insist, accurately be called an epidemic, since its incidence in America has remained fairly constant—and in places even declined—over the past several years. And, while shootings of any kind are undeniably tragic, far more Americans still die each year from pneumonia and influenza than perish in all—not just gun related— homicides and suicides combined.

Not that Christoffel and her colleagues can be bothered by such niggling matters of semantics. What really counts for them is "the data." And the data, they say, show that guns in the hands of the American public are too dangerous to justify whatever redeeming uses they might have. Except that the data *don't* necessarily show that. When doctors venture into the realms of social science and political advocacy, it turns out, their statistics can be as mushy as their definitions.

Consider what is perhaps the most commonly quoted statistic of the gun-control movement—that "a gun at home is 43 times more likely to be used to kill a family member or friend than a criminal intruder." Christoffel and others promoting the "public health approach to handgun violence" use this factoid to convince their patients that keeping a gun in the house is not only

futile as a means of self-defense, it is almost equivalent to sign-
ing the death warrant of a loved one.

Scary stuff, only it's not exactly true. For starters, the study
from which this handy number is derived, printed in a 1986
New England Journal of Medicine article, includes suicides among the
"family members or friends" slain with firearms kept in the
home. Considerably more Americans kill themselves with guns
each year than are murdered with guns, so this is a significant
addition. While doubtless some suicides are impulsive acts, it's
not clear that keeping handguns out of homes would prevent
many people from taking their own lives. Some of the countries
with the world's strictest gun-control laws—Japan, Hungary,
Cuba—also have the highest rates of suicide.

MEDICAL MALPRACTICE

Violence isn't a matter of ordinary people killing because a firearm is handy, but of criminals committing violence because violence is their way of life. When the Centers for Disease Control
starts defining bullets as "pathogens" and brands honest gun
owners the Typhoid Marys of a "gun-violence epidemic," the
medical profession has lent its scientific credibility to a radical
political agenda which threatens to increase the overall violence
in our society by shifting the balance of power toward the well-
armed psychopath.

J. Neil Schulman, *National Review*, May 2, 1994.

The major problem with the statistic, however, is that it measures self-defense by the number of "criminal intruders" killed.
In real life, homeowners use handguns much more often as de-
terrents than as means of deadly force; usually, no shot is fired.
Research conducted by criminologist Gary Kleck found that
each year citizens use firearms to defend themselves more than
2 million times. In only about one of every 1,000 instances is
the attacker shot and killed. A body count, then, is no indication
of whether keeping a gun is a good idea.

INTERPRETING THE DATA

Even when the gun-related data are sound, there's no guarantee
physicians will interpret them in a way consistent with responsible social science. In a 1994 paper in *Pediatrics*, for instance,
Christoffel presented research indicating that white, middle-
class, two-parent families in rural areas were far more likely to
keep a gun in the house than black single mothers with limited

education who lived in the inner city. In other words, Christoffel's data showed, gun ownership was most common among people and in places associated with the country's lowest rates of violent crime. The most violent areas had the fewest reported guns at home.

Statistics like these should be enough to make any gun-control advocate rethink her assumptions about whether gun ownership leads to violence. But not Christoffel. Instead, she advises that "pediatricians treating families with the highest likelihood of [gun] exposure (rural single-family homes, white mothers, adult males present, few preschoolers) should strongly consider incorporating household firearms into anticipatory guidance discussions." As if the Americans most in need of a stern talking-to about gun violence were farmers.

With conclusions like these, it is no surprise that a 1995 review of medical literature on guns and public health published in the *Tennessee Law Review* found that many studies "are so biased and contain so many errors of fact, logic and procedure that we cannot regard them as having a legitimate claim to be treated as scholarly or scientific literature." Edgar Suter, an emergency physician in San Francisco's East Bay who has written about the medical establishment's foray into gun policy, agrees. "There are things being done in the medical literature on guns and violence that strain and even contravene all the canons of scientific integrity, much less of scientific methodology," says Suter. "We also have outright fabrication of data sets."

SLOPPY REASONING

How could physicians—trained to be scrupulously precise and objective—get so sloppy when it comes to facts about guns? When emotions are involved, it's easy. Deborah Prothrow-Stith, dean of the Harvard School of Public Health, comes close to admitting as much in her book. "My own view on gun control is simple," she writes. "I hate guns and I cannot imagine why anybody would want to own one. If I had my way, guns for sport would be registered, and all other guns would be banned." So much for the scientific method.

For a better sense of why otherwise sensible physicians would go out of their way to advise the public on subjects they know little about, it's worth taking a look at the American Academy of Pediatrics, the most radically anti-gun of the major medical associations. Agitating for gun control, it soon becomes clear, is part of a larger pattern of Naderesque finger-wagging. The group takes generally left-of-center positions on just about every trendy subject imaginable, from sexual harassment, corporal punishment, and welfare reform to the 55 mile-per-hour speed limit. The group's nannyish instincts really run amok when it comes to warning parents about the dangers of skateboards, pick-up trucks, snowmobiles, trampolines, bicycles, horseback riding, all-terrain vehicles, ride-on lawn mowers, and, most recently, shopping carts. If there was ever an organization on the lookout for a new "national epidemic," this is it.

BAD MEDICINE

Arthur Kellermann's 1993 study, "Gun Ownership as a Risk Factor for Homicide in the Home," appeared in the *New England Journal of Medicine* (NEJM), a publication known for its anti-gun bias.

Kellermann's principal, widely publicized finding was that if you keep a gun in the home, you are nearly three times more likely to experience a homicide there than if you did not. This finding was peddled unquestioned by the national media.

In a letter to the *NEJM*, David N. Cowan, Ph.D., charged that Kellermann used inappropriate analytic research methods in grouping together socially dysfunctional people (persons, for example, who deal drugs) with "normal" people when he should have used separate analysis for the different groups. The fatal flaw, however, is that only homicide data is evaluated, while the overwhelming majority of protective uses of firearms do not involve anyone being killed.

James Jay Baker, *American Rifleman*, February 1994.

Why, then, does anybody listen to these self-appointed gun experts? The short answer: Because they're doctors. As a paper from the Center to Prevent Handgun Violence shrewdly points out, "Doctors are among the most asked—and trusted—sources of child safety information." And a lot more. Even to a skeptical public, a physician's judgment—on just about any subject—carries considerable weight. All doctors know it; ideological doctors use it.

DOCTOR TO THE WORLD?

According to literature produced by Handgun Control Inc., for example, pediatricians are more than simply good at being doctors, they're also crackerjack sociologists, shrinks, and criminologists. "Doctors are experts in child and adolescent behavior," the pamphlet advises, "and can give parents clear-cut steps to reduce the chances of unintentional and intentional (assaults, homicides, and suicides) gun incidents." Dr. Katherine Christof-fel must have taken this assertion to heart. "I have good creden-tials," she says modestly, "both as a child advocate and an epi-demiologist." From there it's a natural progression to larger callings. "To the extent that I'm an epidemiologist and a public health official," she says, "my patient is the population." Doctor to the world.

For those who would wonder aloud about the seemliness of a physician's pronouncing outside his or her field of expertise, the response can be swift and stinging. In a remarkable November 1995 op-ed in the *Washington Post*, David Satcher, director of the Centers for Disease Control and Prevention, responded to attacks by the National Rifle Association, which had challenged the ac-curacy of CDC studies on gun violence.

"Of all people in our society," Satcher wrote, sounding bewil-dered and angry, "few are more dedicated to intellectual pro-bity—to seeing things as they are—than scientists; it is, in fact, their life's work. If we question the honesty of scientists who give every evidence of long deliberation on the issues before them, what are our expectations of anyone else? What hope is there for us as a society?"

In other words, challenge this research and America itself falls apart. Could anybody but a doctor get away with a state-ment so nakedly self-serving? If the head of the plumbers' union wrote a piece chastising anyone who dared "question the honesty" of plumbers, would people take it seriously? Would the *Post* even print it?

A COMPLICATED ARGUMENT

No matter. The physicians churn out a seemingly endless series of op-eds, though it is not clear that they are adding much to the debate. The arguments that surround gun violence are com-plicated, the obvious conclusions often less obvious than they appear. Perhaps it is a subject that, as a doctor might say, is best left to the experts.

"The appearance and growth of young children on the list of [gun] casualties [is] a nationwide tragedy."

CHILDREN ARE AT RISK FROM HANDGUN VIOLENCE

Clarence Page

More and more American children are becoming victims of handgun violence, maintains Clarence Page in the following viewpoint. Other children, he contends, are traumatized by the gun-related deaths of their classmates or relatives and by the increasing level of violence in their neighborhoods. Page argues that stricter gun-control laws should be implemented to protect the nation's children. Page is a nationally syndicated columnist.

As you read, consider the following questions:

1. According to Page, what is "compassion fatigue"?
2. In the author's opinion, why is a "blame-the-user" approach to gun control ineffective?
3. What measures has Doug Wilder proposed to combat gun violence, according to Page?

Clarence Page, "While Gun Debate Rages On and On," *Washington Times*, January 16, 1993; © Tribune Media Services. Reprinted with permission.

Like other middle-class Chicagoans, Arwilda Burton was shocked by the news that seven bodies had been found in the meat locker of a chicken and pasta restaurant franchise.

In numbers, it was the equivalent of Chicago's legendary St. Valentine's Day Massacre. But this time it was in Palatine, one of the suburbs to which Chicagoans have fled in great numbers to escape urban violence, and two of the victims this time were teenagers.

So Arwilda Burton was shocked, like other middle-class Chicagoans, but she says she also felt the twinges of an additional emotion:

"Empathy," she said. "I understand what the children of that community are going through."

Miss Burton, a social worker, counsels children at the Jenner Elementary School, which services Chicago's crime-plagued Cabrini-Green public housing complex, about 20 miles and a world away from Palatine.

A CHILD'S WORRIES

Cabrini-Green made national news when Dantrell Davis became its third child in 1992 to be fatally shot in sniper cross-fire.

While teams of social workers, psychologists and other grief counselors descended on Palatine High School, which the two slain teens attended, Arwilda Burton helps grade school children at Jenner School deal with similar shocks every week.

One little boy, who lost his brother to gang-related gunfire, loses sleep at night contemplating revenge against the youth accused of the slaying. A small girl copes with the loss of a mother whose body was found in a drainage ditch. Another tries to deal with the violent death of a grandmother and an uncle.

"They are not children as I used to know children," says Miss Burton. "They are not carefree."

The equivalent of the St. Valentine's Day Massacre is happening in Chicago every couple of days in one neighborhood or another. The residents of high-crime neighborhoods never get used to the violence that churns all around them. But the rest of us seem to get a little too easily accustomed to hearing about or, for that matter, to caring about it.

"Compassion fatigue" is the fashionable term, even though heaven knows we have not done much to feel fatigued about. We are more quickly moved by the few deaths close to home that we can comprehend than by the many deaths a little farther removed from our daily lives. Joseph Stalin understood this curious side of human nature when he declared, "A single death is a tragedy; a million deaths is a statistic."

It is hard to comprehend the massive numbers of handgun-related deaths in America (22,000 Americans from 1990 to 1992 alone). But a glimpse into the world of Arwilda Burton should cause us to stop, for a moment, to consider a horrible new development: the appearance and growth of young children on the list of casualties.

It's a nationwide tragedy. Los Angeles King/Drew Medical Center, for example, which had not admitted a single child under 10 years of age for gunshot wounds before 1980, admitted 34 between 1980 and 1987.

Copyright 1993 by Herblock in the *Washington Post*. Reprinted with permission.

But what can we do about it? We might not be able to stop all such violence, but we can at least close gaping holes in the laws that control the sale and distribution of guns in America, where the homicide rate dwarfs that of the rest of the industrialized— and civilized—world.

The National Rifle Association, which never saw a gun-control law it liked, argues that we don't need new gun-control laws. Instead they say we need only to enforce existing laws with tougher sentences for anyone who uses a gun to break the law.

But that blame-the-users approach is a cop-out, since existing laws leave gaping loopholes for gunmakers, dealers and distributors to make a killing, figuratively and literally, by making and selling guns to unlawful or irresponsible people.

In "The Story of a Gun" an eye-opening examination of today's gun trade in the January 1993 *Atlantic* magazine, writer Erik Larson describes how "a none-of-my-business attitude permeates the firearms distribution chain from production to final sale allowing gunmakers and gun marketers to promote the killing power of their weapons while disavowing any responsibility for their use in crime."

Mr. Larson, who says he does not oppose guns, not even handguns, in the hands of responsible owners, describes how mass killers like Nicholas Elliot, 16, who shot up Atlantic Shores Christian School, in Virginia Beach in 1988, acquired their weapons through federally licensed dealers, using a means "that existing federal gun-trade regulations do much to encourage."

Yet, what happens when lawmakers try to impose even the slightest impediment on the gun flow? The NRA goes, well, ballistic, unleashing massive amounts of campaign donations, then calling in the IOUs, stopping reform in its tracks.

A MODEST PROPOSAL

Virginia Gov. Doug Wilder, whose state may be the biggest single supplier of guns trafficked up and down the Eastern Seaboard, has proposed limiting gun purchases to one per month per individual. It's a modest proposal, yet the NRA vows to fight it. Mr. Wilder, a veteran of many legislative battles, expects "the biggest fight I've ever encountered."

Amazing. Sometimes I wonder how those who knowingly supply heavy weapons and silencers to kids, gangsters and crackpots manage to sleep at night. But I wonder even more how the rest of us can sleep at night, knowing that we could put a pinch on the traffic yet do nothing. Apathy is killing us.

| "Gun accidents involving both children
and adults have actually fallen
dramatically since the 1970s."

CHILDREN ARE NOT AT RISK FROM HANDGUN VIOLENCE

David B. Kopel

David B. Kopel is the director of the Second Amendment Project at the Independence Institute, a think tank that supports gun ownership as a civil liberty. In the following viewpoint, Kopel argues that gun-control advocates exaggerate children's risk from handguns. Children who are properly taught gun-safety measures are less likely to be involved in gun-related accidents or with crime, he contends. Therefore, Kopel maintains, the key to reducing the risk of gun violence for children is to teach them responsible firearm use.

As you read, consider the following questions:
1. How many Americans under the age of twenty were murdered in 1991, according to Kopel?
2. In Kopel's opinion, how do proposals that advocate "do it for our kids" affect discussion of gun-control laws?
3. According to the author, how have firearm safety programs affected the incidence of gun accidents since the 1970s?

From David B. Kopel, "Gun Play." Reprinted, with permission, from the July 1993 issue of *Reason* magazine. Copyright 1993 by the Reason Foundation, 3415 S. Sepulveda Blvd., Suite 400, Los Angeles, CA 90034.

"Too many kids are getting a real bang out of life," announced a full-page ad in the New York Times. "Help save the next generation." The body text elaborates: "Too many kids are becoming victims of gun violence. Every day in the United States, 14 children are killed with guns—in accidents, suicides and homicides. Hundreds more are injured—many seriously."

Beneath the main headline is a photograph of Jim Brady, the former White House press secretary who was wounded and disabled in John Hinckley's attempted assassination of President Reagan. (The ad appeared on March 30, 1993, the 12th anniversary of Hinckley's attack.) Brady's picture is flanked by quotes from urban kids discussing their fears of gun violence. The text below his picture implores Americans to support the so-called Brady Bill, which would impose a nationwide, seven-day waiting period for handgun purchases. "I'm not asking you to do it for me," Brady says. "But do it for our kids."

The ad, purchased by Handgun Control Inc., reflects the theme of the organization's latest push for the Brady Bill. [The bill was signed into law by Bill Clinton in November 1993.] In a February 1993 press conference, Sarah Brady, Jim Brady's wife and Handgun Control's chairwoman, noted that nearly 4,000 Americans under the age of 20 had been murdered in 1991. (That number, actually closer to 3,700, covers a lot of ground. It's based on arrests, so it includes 18-year-old armed robbers shot by their victims. It also includes 19-year-old crack dealers shot by competitors.) Acting Attorney General Stewart Gerson added that the Department of Justice endorsed the Brady Bill because he was sick of seeing kids gunned down in random violence.

NO IMPACT ON CRIME

Neither Brady nor Gerson suggested how many lives the Brady Bill might save. Nor did they cite studies showing how similar laws, enacted by more than 20 states, have reduced crime. That's because there are no such studies. All the scholarly research has found that laws like the Brady Bill have no statistically significant impact on crime.

But the whole idea of asking people to "do it for our kids" is to avoid such analysis. Gun-control advocates are hammering at the issue of children and guns as never before in the hope that it will be easier to enact gun controls aimed at adults in an atmosphere of panic about children. Sen. John Chafee (R-R.I.), for example, says firearms are "infecting" America's schools; he has proposed the confiscation of all civilian-owned handguns. Chafee insists that America must "do something" about the current "handgun slaughter," in which "our children are being killed and are killing," for "sooner rather than later every family in the U.S. will be touched by handgun violence." His confiscation legislation won immediate support from "prochild" lobbies such as the Children's Defense Fund and the American Academy of Pediatrics.

THE DECLINE IN ACCIDENTAL CHILDHOOD GUN DEATHS

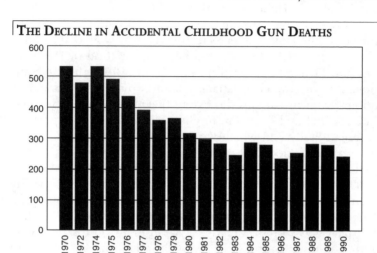

Source: National Safety Council's *Accident Facts* and the National Center for Health Statistics.

The idea of curtailing the rights of adults to protect children is hardly new to American politics. Prohibitionists have used this tactic in arguing for bans on alcohol, marijuana, sexually explicit literature, homosexual behavior, lawn darts, and just about everything else they have ever sought to outlaw. It's precisely because such efforts have so often been successful that the talk about protecting children through gun control should not be dismissed as mere rhetoric. Threats to children, whether real or imagined, tend to short-circuit rational discussion. Gun-control proposals should not escape critical examination simply because their supporters paint a horrifying picture of children at risk.

A SERIOUS PROBLEM

America does have a serious problem with children and guns, but it's a problem quite different from the one described by America's gun prohibitionists and their Washington allies. Indeed, it's a problem that has been aggravated by anti-gun laws.

Consider how the repressive gun laws of cities such as Chicago, Washington, and New York drive responsible gun use underground. While a man who operates a bodega on the Lower East

Side of New York City may keep an illegal pistol hidden under the counter in case of a robbery, he is not likely to take the gun to a target range for practice. Even if the storekeeper managed to get a gun license, he could not take his teenage son to a target range to teach him responsible firearm use. Just to hold the gun in his hand under immediate adult supervision at a licensed range, the teenager would have to obtain his own permit.

An airgun, which uses compressed air to shoot a pellet, is safe enough to fire inside an apartment, yet New York City makes it illegal for supervised minors to touch one. The city thus closes off one more avenue for children to be taught proper firearm use.

Research suggests that the loss of these opportunities makes a difference. In a 1991 study of 675 ninth- and 10th-graders in Rochester, New York, for example, the children who were taught about guns by their families were at no greater risk of becoming involved in crime, gangs, or drugs than children with no exposure to guns. But the children who were taught about guns by their peers were considerably more likely to be involved in various kinds of misbehavior, including gun crime. A study of whites and aborigines in northwest Australia in the late '80s yielded a similar result: Young men who were taught about guns by responsible authority figures did not commit gun crimes, even if they broke the law in other ways.

In this light, repressive gun laws are not merely ineffective. They actually foster misuse of firearms, including gun violence. By making firearm ownership illegal, or possible only for wealthy people with the clout to move through numerous bureaucratic obstacles, anti-gun laws render legitimate gun owners invisible. Children are left with criminals and violent television characters as their only models of gun use. In cities where no child may shoot a BB gun with his parent, kids learn about firearms on the street and shoot each other with 9-mm pistols.

THE IMPORTANCE OF FIREARM LESSONS

The experience with gun accidents shows the importance of teaching our children about proper firearm use. Gun-control advocates have sought to create the impression that firearm accidents involving children are a large and growing problem. Paradoxically, this impression has been reinforced by the very fact that such accidents are rare. Almost every time a child dies in a gun accident, the event is covered by the state's wire services, and sometimes by the national news. Many people mistakenly conclude that children die frequently in gun accidents and that sharp restrictions on gun ownership are necessary to address the problem. But gun accidents involving both children and adults have actually fallen dramatically since the 1970s, almost entirely because of private safety efforts.

In 1988, 277 children under the age of 15 were killed by accidental firearm discharges, according to the National Safety Council. That number represents a 48 percent drop from 1974, even as the number of guns per capita increased. From 1968 to 1988, the annual rate of fatal gun accidents fell from 1.2 per 100,000 Americans to 0.6. Thanks to private educational efforts, including programs sponsored by the National Rifle Association, the Boy Scouts, 4-H, and other groups, the firearm accident rate has been cut in half.

FATAL ACCIDENTS AMONG U.S. CHILDREN AGES 0 TO 14: 1991

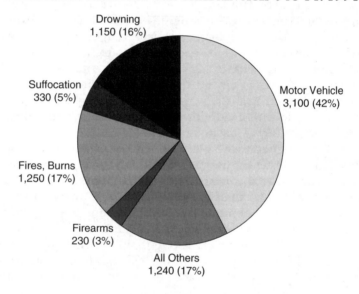

Drowning
1,150 (16%)

Suffocation
330 (5%)

Motor Vehicle
3,100 (42%)

Fires, Burns
1,250 (17%)

Firearms
230 (3%)

All Others
1,240 (17%)

All Fatal Accidents: 7,300

Source: National Safety Council.

Despite this impressive private-sector achievement, Sen. Howard Metzenbaum (D-Ohio) thinks that the government could do better. He proposes giving the Consumer Product Safety Commission authority over firearms, ostensibly to reduce accidents. This move could be an indirect way to achieve gun controls far more sweeping and restrictive than Congress is likely to pass. With jurisdiction over firearms, the CPSC could, by unilateral administrative action, ban the future production and sale of all firearms and ammunition. Congress has forbidden the CPSC to regulate guns precisely because of such fears.

Short of banning firearms, the CPSC might require features intended to prevent accidents, such as child-proof grips or indicators that show when a gun is loaded. But such technological fixes, favorites of the gun-control lobby, do not address the main cause of firearm accidents. A 1991 study by the General Accounting Office found that 84 percent of gun accidents involve deviations from basic safety rules. For example, accidents occur when people carelessly wave a gun around, thinking it's unloaded, or put their fingers on the trigger prematurely. Safety education is therefore the best way to continue reducing gun accidents. Unfortunately, children whose parents have no interest in firearms are unlikely to hear gun lessons. Firearm-safety programs ought to be expanded to reach more children.

GUN SAFETY PROGRAMS

One successful effort to teach children about gun safety is the NRA's "Eddie Eagle" Elementary Gun Safety Education Program. The Eddie Eagle program offers curricula for children from kindergarten through sixth grade, using an animated video, cartoon workbooks, and play safety activities. The cartoon hero Eddie Eagle offers a simple safety lesson: "If you see a gun: Stop! Don't Touch. Leave the Area. Tell an Adult." Although Eddie Eagle includes no political content, some anti-gun activists have prevented the program from being used in their schools because they disagree with the NRA's position on policy issues. (Riflery programs in high schools, which also teach safe gun habits, have generated even more resistance.)

While schools and other social institutions have an important role to play in gun safety, the primary responsibility rests with parents. A child who can, under parental supervision, invite a classmate to shoot a .22 rifle at a target range will be less intrigued by the possibility of surreptitiously playing with a pistol found in a closet.

PERIODICAL BIBLIOGRAPHY

The following articles have been selected to supplement the diverse views presented in this chapter. Addresses are provided for periodicals not indexed in the *Readers' Guide to Periodical Literature*, the *Alternative Press Index*, the *Social Sciences Index*, or the *Index to Legal Periodicals and Books*.

James Jay Baker — "Gun Control Is Bad Medicine," *American Rifleman*, February 1994. Available from 11250 Waples Mill Rd., Fairfax, VA 22030.

John Berendt — "The Gun," *Esquire*, September 1993.

Michael Hill — "Well-Regulated Militia," *Chronicles*, March 1995. Available from 934 N. Main St., Rockford, IL 61103-7061.

Arthur L. Kellermann et al. — "Gun Ownership as a Risk Factor for Homicide in the Home," *New England Journal of Medicine*, October 7, 1993. Available from 10 Shattuck St., Boston, MA 02115-6094.

Charles Marwick — "A Public Health Approach to Making Guns Safer," *JAMA*, June 14, 1995. Available from 515 N. State St., Chicago, IL 60610.

Roger D. McGrath — "Treat Them to a Good Dose of Lead," *Chronicles*, January 1994.

Daniel D. Polsby — "The False Promise of Gun Control," *Atlantic Monthly*, March 1994.

Roy Romer — "Guns in the Hands of Kids," *Vital Speeches of the Day*, November 1, 1993.

Susan H. Schoolfield — "Can Children and Guns Coexist in the Home?" *USA Today*, January 1994.

Jacob Sullum — "What the Doctor Orders," *Reason*, January 1996.

Barbara Vobejda — "There's No Place Like Homicide," *Washington Post National Weekly Edition*, October 25–31, 1993.

James D. Wright — "Ten Essential Observations on Guns in America," *Society*, March/April 1995.

CHAPTER 2

DOES THE CONSTITUTION PROTECT PRIVATE GUN OWNERSHIP?

CHAPTER PREFACE

In the summer of 1993, after several children fell out of windows at Chicago public housing complexes, the Chicago Housing Authority (CHA) decided to install window guards. When CHA workers attempted to enter the buildings, however, they were fired upon by gang members with semiautomatic weapons. Vincent Lane, chairman of the CHA, was outraged at this attack on the repair crews and organized a gun sweep in the housing development. He defended his actions by comparing the random gunfire at the complex to a bomb threat: "When there's a threat of a bomb and you don't know where it is, you look everywhere you can; you don't run and get a search warrant before you look for the bomb." To prevent the searches from being called illegal, CHA workers inspected the apartments for physical problems that needed to be repaired. During their inspections the searchers found and confiscated numerous weapons ranging from .45-mm pistols to MAC-10 semiautomatic rifles and high-powered rifles with scopes. Lane was enthusiastic about the search and its results: "The weapons we took out of the building could do a lot of damage on the street in the wrong hands."

The American Civil Liberties Union (ACLU) felt differently about the search for guns, however. It filed suit in federal court to stop the weapons sweep, calling it a violation of the Fourth Amendment's prohibition against unlawful search and seizure. ACLU lawyers argued that since residents of the luxury high-rise apartments overlooking Chicago's lakefront would not be expected to tolerate such intrusions, neither should public housing tenants. Gun sweeps are not the answer to reducing violence, maintains Harvey M. Grossman, ACLU's legal director. "We believe adequate, competent law enforcement is the answer. We don't want less security. We want more security." U.S. district judge Wayne Anderson agreed with the ACLU and ruled the sweeps unconstitutional in April 1994.

Gun sweeps are not the only form of gun control opposed on constitutional grounds. Indeed, questions about the meaning of the Second Amendment are at the heart of the argument over gun control. Gun-rights advocates maintain that the amendment guarantees every individual the right to own a firearm without restrictions. Gun-control supporters contend that the Second Amendment's guarantee refers to state-supported militias, not to individuals. The authors in the following chapter debate the meaning of the Second Amendment and whether it permits gun control.

"American citizens—and not the states—have a right to keep and bear arms which may not be infringed."

PRIVATE GUN OWNERSHIP IS PROTECTED BY THE SECOND AMENDMENT

Steven Silver

Steven Silver maintains in the following viewpoint that the Second Amendment guarantees individuals the inalienable right to keep and bear arms. If the framers of the Second Amendment had intended to grant states the power to maintain militias, he contends, they would have worded the amendment to clearly express this. However, he argues, the Second Amendment specifically grants the right to the people and therefore protects individuals' right of private ownership. Silver is a contributing editor to the *Firearms Sentinel* and is vice president of the Lawyer's Second Amendment Society, an organization that supports gun ownership rights.

As you read, consider the following questions:

1. According to the author, what is the difference between a "right" and a "power"?
2. According to Silver, why is the ACLU's claim that the National Guard is the modern-day equivalent of the militia absurd?
3. What prevents the Supreme Court from repealing the Second Amendment, in Silver's opinion?

From Steven Silver, "Dishonesty and Deception: The ACLU and the Second Amendment," *Firearms Sentinel*, Fall/Winter 1995. Reprinted by permission of the author.

The American Civil Liberties Union is, by far, the leading American civil rights organization. For decades, it has championed the cause of American citizens against the ever-encroaching power of the government.

The ACLU has worked to defend Americans' rights under the First, Fourth and Fifth Amendments. Indeed, the ACLU has worked to free those convicted of murder because of minor technical irregularities during their arrests. It has also defended the right of avowed racists and anti-Semites to march in public.

Surprisingly, the ACLU has entirely ignored arguably one of the most important rights guaranteed in the Bill of Rights; namely, the individual's right to keep and bear arms, recognized in the Second Amendment. What can explain this anomaly?

THE ACLU's POSITION

The ACLU explains this contradiction simply by relying upon *U.S. v. Miller*, a narrow decision issued by the Supreme Court in 1939. The ACLU states its position on the Second Amendment is "well known and not subject to change." The ACLU believes the right to keep and bear arms is an anachronistic protection of the right of the states to maintain militias, and thereby to insure the states' "freedom" and security against the Federal government.

Superficially, this argument seems to make sense. The Second Amendment clearly refers to the necessity for a "well regulated Militia." But after further consideration, obviously necessary when our civil rights are on the block, it quickly becomes clear the ACLU's position is based on errors and illogic. . . .

THE SECOND AMENDMENT'S MEANING

The best place to begin to determine the meaning of the Second Amendment is to focus on the language of the Amendment itself: "A well regulated Militia, being necessary to the security of a free State, the right of the people to keep and bear Arms, shall not be infringed."

Note that the Amendment does not say states may keep and bear arms. Rather, it says the "people" may do so. In 1990, the Supreme Court, in *U.S. v. Verdugo-Urquidez*, declared that the term "people" used in the Bill of Rights means that "class of persons who are part of the national community. . . ."

If the Supreme Court's definition of the word "people" is inserted into the Amendment, its meaning becomes perhaps clearer: "A well regulated Militia, being necessary to the security of a free State, the right of that class of persons who are part of the national community to keep and bear Arms, shall not be infringed."

Better yet, since the "class of persons who are part of the national community" simply means American citizens, the meaning of the Second Amendment can be further clarified as follows: "A well regulated Militia, being necessary to the security of a free State, the right of American citizens to keep and bear Arms, shall not be infringed."

This simple exercise makes it quite clear that, regardless of the meaning of the reference to the Militia, American citizens—and not the states—have a right to keep and bear arms which may not be infringed.

THE MILITIA IS THE PEOPLE

When the Constitution means "states" it says so. . . . The ultimate right to keep and bear arms belongs to "the people," not the "states.". . . Thus the "people" at the core of the Second Amendment [a]re [the] Citizens—the same "We the People" who "ordain and establish" the Constitution and whose right to assemble . . . [is] at the core of the First Amendment. . . . Nowadays, it is quite common to speak loosely of the National Guard as "the state militia," but [when the Second Amendment was written] . . . "the militia" referred to all Citizens capable of bearing arms. [Thus] "the militia" is identical to "the people."

Akhil Amar, *Yale Law Journal*, March 1991.

Indeed, it is not clear what part of the phrase, "the right of the people to keep and bear Arms shall not be infringed," the ACLU does not understand. It certainly requires some mental gymnastics helped by dubious logic for the ACLU to conclude the right of the people to keep and bear arms may be infringed by the government.

It is also curious that, despite the simple language in the Second Amendment which plainly means all Americans have an inalienable right to keep and bear arms, the ACLU refuses to acknowledge the Amendment guarantees such an individual right. Yet, the ACLU has no trouble finding a "fundamental," yet unwritten, right of privacy, including a right to abortion, floating around somewhere in the nebulous "penumbra" of the Constitution. . . .

THE FRAMERS' INTENT

Since the language used in the Second Amendment inescapably means that individuals have a right to own firearms, the ACLU must fall back on the argument that the Amendment was intended only to provide for a militia. Yet, there is not a single shred of evidence from the Constitutional Convention which supports this proposition. "Gun control" proponents have yet to identify even a single quote from one of the Founders to support their claim.

Mountainous evidence, including quotations from the Framers' writings, makes it absolutely clear they intended the Second Amendment to recognize an individual right. The ACLU's "collective" rights theory is a creation of the 20th century; it was unknown in the 1700s.

Indeed, the Framers were themselves armed with state-of-the-art military firearms. We know what happened to the British when they were foolish enough to suggest that American colonists did not have the right to keep and bear arms. British troops marched through Lexington, Massachusetts, on their way to Concord to seize the Americans' weapons and powder. That seizure effort touched off the Revolution.

Further, virtually all legitimate academic research regarding the Second Amendment indicates it was intended to recognize an individual right. Of 42 law review articles which addressed the Second Amendment since 1980, all but five concluded it guaranteed an individual right. Of these five, three were written by "researchers" hired by anti-gun groups; one was written by a politician!

Even the American Bar Association had to acknowledge in its 1965 article, "The Lost Amendment," that the Amendment guaranteed an individual right. Bowing to political pressure, the ABA now asserts the Amendment guarantees only a state's right to maintain a militia.

THE SUPREME COURT'S INTERPRETATION

In the often-cited cases of *Cruikshank v. U.S.* and *Presser v. Illinois*, 1875 and 1885, respectively, the Supreme Court stated the Second Amendment did not create a right. Rather, the Court expressly recognized a pre-existing right to keep and bear arms.

The Court held that Americans' right to keep and bear arms did not come from the Second Amendment. This is where the ACLU's analysis stops. However, the ACLU always ignores the Court's statement that the Amendment simply recognizes a pre-existing right.

This distinction is the crux of the individual rights position. The ACLU disingenuously asserts the Amendment did not create a right. True enough. But, as the Court stated, that right exists, and it existed before the Bill of Rights was ratified. All that document did was to state that the right would not be infringed by the government. . . .

STATES DO NOT HAVE "RIGHTS"

Under Article I of the U.S. Constitution, and the Tenth Amendment, "powers" are reserved to the States. By contrast, American citizens have "rights."

A right is a fundamental quality of life which resides in each individual, such as life, liberty and pursuit of happiness. Indeed, it was the British Crown's denial of Americans' inalienable rights which gave rise to the Declaration of Independence.

Certainly, states cannot enjoy the rights of life, liberty and pursuit of happiness. A state is not a living being. It cannot exercise liberty (just as its liberty cannot be taken away by incarceration). Similarly, a state cannot pursue happiness. Only individuals can exercise these "rights."

In short, a "collective" right is not a right at all. It is simply a "power." Since the Second Amendment guarantees a "right" of the people, by definition it is a right which may be exercised only by individual citizens, and not by states.

For this reason, the ACLU's claim that the Second Amendment guarantees a "collective" right, intended to assure the states' "freedom," is absurd.

It is also worthwhile to note that the First, Third, Fourth, Fifth, Sixth, Seventh and Eighth Amendments also expressly guarantee rights which can only be exercised by individual citizens. It is nonsensical to conclude the Second Amendment— alone in the Bill of Rights—does not pertain to individuals.

THE MILITIA REFERENCE

Based on the first clause of the Second Amendment, the ACLU suggests the Second Amendment guarantees only a state's right to maintain a militia. This, too, is a misinterpretation of the history and meaning of the Amendment.

During the Revolutionary era, every city and township maintained its own militia. There were also private militias. In Lexington, Massachusetts, it was the town militia which squared off against the British regulars.

Historically, and under current law, militias consisted of "citizen-soldiers." This meant all able-bodied males between 18 and 45 years old were expected to muster, bearing their own arms, during times of threat. Today all able-bodied citizens of either sex would probably be expected so to appear.

Since a militia consisted of all the armed citizens, it could exist only if all the citizens were armed. For this reason, the ACLU's assertion that the reference to a "well regulated Militia" confers a right upon the states is, again, ludicrous.

In addition, the term "well regulated" meant "well disciplined," and not regulated by the state. Indeed, soldiers of the day were referred to as "regulars." It is a little-known fact that on his famous ride in 1775, Paul Revere did not yell, "The British are coming!" as commonly is believed. Rather, he yelled: "The Regulars are coming!"

THE RIGHT OF THE PEOPLE

The phrase "the right of the people" is used elsewhere in the Bill of Rights to guarantee the right of individuals. The First Amendment refers to "the right of the people peaceably to assemble, and to petition the Government for a redress of grievances." The Fourth Amendment refers to "the right of the people to be secure in their persons, houses, papers, and effects, against unreasonable searches and seizures. . . ." The authors of the Bill of Rights surely would not have used the phrase "the right of the people" to mean the rights of individuals in some amendments, while using that same phrase in other amendments to mean the right of the collective, which in essence means the right of government.

Gary Benoit, *New American*, April 4, 1994.

The ACLU's claim that the National Guard is the modern-day equivalent of the militia is equally absurd. Were the National Guard and militias synonymous, then every state with a National Guard unit would be in violation of Art. I, Section 10, Clause 3 of the U.S. Constitution. which forbids the states from raising armies in peace time.

The Framers were all very smart. If they intended the Amendment to guarantee states' power to maintain militias, they would have said so. They would not have acknowledged the "people's" right to be armed if they did not intend to provide for that. Under the ACLU's reading, the entire second portion of the Amendment, the part which actually states the right, is meaningless and to no effect.

INALIENABLE RIGHTS

The ACLU frequently asserts we should ignore the Amendment's plain meaning because no court has expressly said the Amendment guarantees an individual right. This statement is basically true. But it also poses fundamental problems: Where do our rights come from? Can they be eliminated? If rights can be eliminated, then they are not inalienable.

The Supreme Court often makes "mistakes." In *Plessy v. Ferguson* (1897), the Court held the "separate but equal" doctrine was consistent with the Fourteenth Amendment. Fifty years later, in 1954, the Court held in *Brown v. Board of Education* that the "separate but equal" doctrine was invalid under the Fourteenth Amendment.

The Supreme Court once recognized that some citizens could have a property right in other human beings, because slavery was accepted for nearly 100 years in this country.

The ACLU would surely not accept that Congress's enactment of a law that prohibited anti-government speech because it made governing too difficult—and the Court upheld that law—could nullify the First Amendment.

The ACLU would be right to object to such a law: Neither Congress nor the Court could repeal the protections offered by the First Amendment. The same goes for the Second Amendment.

Our rights exist independent of the very government against which the Bill of Rights is asserted. That's why they are called rights.

The Supreme Court may properly try to determine if a restriction on a right is reasonable, since no right is absolute. But the Court has no legislative powers, and thus no authority to repeal a right. Indeed, it is doubtful if a "right" could be repealed at all, even by a majority vote of the population. Were this not so, the Thirteenth Amendment could be repealed by popular vote, and slavery re-instituted, which would clearly deprive the victims of their inalienable rights.

The ACLU attempts to confuse the issue with the question: What types of "Arms" are protected by the Second Amendment? Tanks? Bazookas? Machine guns?

The answer is simple. Like any right set forth in the Bill of Rights, the word "Arms" is subject to reasonable limitations so long as the purpose of the Amendment can still be achieved. As Alexander Hamilton stated in Federalist Paper No. 29, the Amendment's purpose historically was to allow American citizens to protect their lives, liberty and pursuit of happiness against foreign or domestic threats, including a large standing army.

Thus, Americans may keep and bear whatever arms are reasonably necessary to protect them from any threat to their life, liberty or pursuit of happiness.

In short, if the ACLU is willing to acknowledge the Second Amendment guarantees a right to every individual American, we can then determine which "reasonable limitations" apply yet still let us achieve the purpose of the Second Amendment.

> "The Second Amendment does not guarantee individuals a right to keep and bear arms for private, non-militia purposes."

PRIVATE GUN OWNERSHIP IS NOT PROTECTED BY THE SECOND AMENDMENT

Los Angeles Times

In the following viewpoint, the editors of the *Los Angeles Times* dispute the contention that the Second Amendment guarantees private gun ownership. The authors of the Second Amendment intended only to grant states the right to maintain militias, the editors contend, and to allow citizens to own guns for use in their militia. Private, non-militia use of firearms is not protected by the Second Amendment, they maintain. The *Times*, in a series of editorials, has advocated a near-total ban on the private possession of handguns.

As you read, consider the following questions:

1. What organization is the modern-day equivalent of a state militia, according to the *Los Angeles Times*?
2. How has the U.S. Supreme Court defined "militia," as quoted by the *Times*?
3. When do gun-control laws violate the Second Amendment, according to the authors?

"Taming the Gun Monster: Is It Constitutional?" *Los Angeles Times* editorial, November 1, 1993. Copyright 1993, Los Angeles Times. Reprinted with permission.

The *Los Angeles Times* supports a near-total ban on handguns and assault weapons, leaving these weapons pretty much only in the hands of law enforcement authorities. Under the *Times'* program—proposed in response to the gun epidemic that is devastating America in general and the Los Angeles area in particular—hunting rifles and sport guns would be kept only by licensed owners who have submitted to a background check and completed training in the safe use of those weapons.

This program . . . prompted hundreds of readers to write in, most expressing support but others expressing opposition. Among those readers who oppose our call for a near-total ban on handguns and automatic weapons, a recurring argument is that the Second Amendment to the Constitution bars tough gun control. They read that amendment as conferring on citizens a right to have firearms. Thus, they say, Congress can't pass stricter gun laws.

Theirs is a frequently used argument. It's a powerful argument. It's an important argument. But there's only one problem: It's a fallacious argument.

WHAT THE AMENDMENT DOES

In its entirety, the Second Amendment states: *A well regulated Militia, being necessary to the security of a free State, the right of the people to keep and bear Arms, shall not be infringed.*

Opponents of stronger gun restrictions maintain that this 27-word amendment confers on private citizens a largely unrestricted right to own a gun. Moreover, they contend that the drafters of the Bill of Rights created this right not merely for the convenience of 18th-Century hunters, or frightened 20th-Century urbanites, but rather as an indispensable element of the democratic tradition—to protect against government tyranny.

Indeed, the Second Amendment has created a significant political impediment to the passage of stronger gun control laws. Gun-ownership advocates argue not that Congress should not, as a matter of policy, enact such laws but rather that Congress cannot do so because the amendment ties its hands.

But did the drafters of the Second Amendment intend it to guarantee a right of all citizens to possess firearms? Many scholars who have analyzed the Constitutional Convention, the state ratification debates and subsequent Second Amendment jurisprudence answer "no." They find, prior to the drafting of the amendment, precious little discussion of a right to have firearms for hunting, target shooting, self-defense or any other purposes unrelated to a state militia. The Second Amendment arose from the colonists' fear of a standing army in the hands of a powerful central government. As they created that new central government—the United States of America—many drafters were unsure whether the states would retain the authority to maintain militias. The amendment responded to that concern and that concern only.

THE HISTORY OF THE STATE MILITIAS

But after ratification of the Constitution and the Bill of Rights, states quickly demonstrated they were incapable of—and largely uninterested in—maintaining their own militias. One legal scholar notes, "The history of the state militias between 1800 and the 1870s is one of total abandonment, disorganization and degeneration." States could not afford to arm their militias, and citizens became impatient with training and duty. States joining the Union had no Revolutionary militia tradition and even less enthusiasm, and money, for organizing their own units. Yet many felt that states should nonetheless retain a military capability.

©Matt Wuerker. Reprinted with permission.

So beginning in 1903 Congress passed the first of several acts designed to fund, equip and organize state militias. These federal efforts have resulted in the National Guard, the present-day state militias. States provide the armories and storage facilities, federal funds provide clothing, weapons and equipment, and the Army and Air Force supervise the training of Guard members. Because no state still requires its citizens to supply weapons for its militia, private weapon possession no longer bears any relationship to an effective militia.

However, many argue that the National Guard should not be viewed as the militia envisioned by drafters of the Second Amendment. They maintain that *militia* means unorganized private citizens with guns who could use them to rise up against a tyrannical government. Yet what is totally remarkable—and underreported and under-appreciated—is that federal courts have not agreed. In fact, the Second Amendment has inspired a remarkable degree of consensus among federal judges: The proposition that the Second Amendment does *not* guarantee individuals a right to keep and bear arms for private, non-militia purposes is among the more firmly established propositions in U.S. constitutional law.

Federal courts have not spoken out often on the issue of gun control—partly because Congress has passed relatively few laws on this subject compared to, say, interstate commerce. But when courts, including the U.S. Supreme Court, have ruled, they have consistently upheld a variety of firearm restrictions, even prohibitions.

DEFINING "MILITIA"

Beginning with a 1939 decision upholding federal restrictions on the possession of a type of shotgun popular with gangsters, the Supreme Court commented specifically on the meaning of the militia clause. In this case, *United States vs. Miller*, the court recognized the right of individuals to possess firearms but created the limitation that the firearms must serve the collective purpose. The court referred to the militia as "a body of citizens enrolled for military discipline"—not as an armed citizenry at large.

Subsequent federal decisions, including rulings in the last few years, consistently have held that federal statutes regulating firearms do not violate the Second Amendment unless they interfere with maintenance of an organized state militia. In practice, this analytical framework has meant that since 1939 no federal gun law has been found to be in conflict with the Second Amendment.

Instead, courts have upheld laws barring convicted felons from transporting guns in interstate commerce, requiring registration of machine guns, imposing licensing and record-keeping requirements on gun dealers and prohibiting firearm purchasers from providing false statements, and even an Illinois ban on possession of most handguns. In these cases, the courts have held that the Second Amendment guarantees a "collective right," not an individual one.

Is the Second Amendment a barrier to tougher federal gun laws? No federal court in the 20th Century has suggested that private ownership of firearms by members of the "sedentary" or "unorganized" militia is protected by the amendment. Instead, federal courts, including the Supreme Court, offer scant solace to absolutists' claims about the right to bear arms.

THE FLOW OF JUDICIAL HISTORY

Would a near-blanket handgun and assault weapon ban of the sort the *Times* proposes be upheld if challenged, as it surely would be? No one can unfailingly predict what any court would decide on any issue, and courts sometimes switch directions dramatically. But if the long jurisprudential history of the Second Amendment is a guide, and it often has been, there is a better than fair chance such a ban would prevail.

Very little in the Constitution is absolute. What's offered is a set of checks and balances, some assurance that the pursuit of happiness can flourish in an environment of relative predictability and justice. Constitutional amendments, because they rarely are absolute, are continuing grist for judicial interpretation. Consider the First Amendment, which provides for a measure of freedom of speech, religion and the press. Those guarantees aren't absolute: While given a wide berth, religion and the press both have to operate within certain limitations. Neither was the Second Amendment designed to be absolute. It does not guarantee a right to bear arms. It certainly was not intended to permit this nation to engage in the deadly firefight that is slaughtering its people.

| "The Constitution of the United States unconditionally protects the people's right to keep and bear arms."

GUN CONTROL IS UNCONSTITUTIONAL

J. Neil Schulman

In the following viewpoint, J. Neil Schulman argues that the Second Amendment guarantees the absolute right of the people to keep and bear arms. The belief that the amendment applies only to well-regulated militias is wrong, Schulman contends. He cites Roy Copperud, an expert in the usage of the English language, who interprets the amendment's wording to mean that an individual's right of gun ownership cannot be restricted in any way. Therefore, Schulman concludes, laws regulating gun ownership are unconstitutional. Schulman is the author of *Stopping Power: Why 70 Million Americans Own Guns.*

As you read, consider the following questions:

1. According to Copperud, as quoted by the author, is the right to keep and bear arms granted by the Second Amendment or is it a pre-existing right?
2. What does the phrase "well-regulated" mean, in Copperud's opinion, as cited by Schulman?
3. What does the author imply that people should do if their right to bear arms is restricted and regulated?

From J. Neil Schulman, "The Text of the Second Amendment," *Journal on Firearms and Public Policy*, Summer 1992. Copyright 1992, the Second Amendment Foundation. Reprinted by permission.

If you wanted to know all about the Big Bang, you'd ring up Carl Sagan, right? And if you wanted to know about desert warfare, the man to call would be Norman Schwartzkopf, no question about it. But who would you call if you wanted the top expert on American usage to tell you the meaning of the Second Amendment to the United States Constitution?

That was the question I asked A.C. Brocki, editorial coordinator of the Los Angeles Unified School District and formerly senior editor at Houghton Mifflin Publishers—who himself had been recommended to me as the foremost expert on English usage in the Los Angeles school system. Mr. Brocki told me to get in touch with Roy Copperud, a retired professor of journalism at the University of Southern California and the author of *American Usage and Style: The Consensus*.

A little research lent support to Brocki's opinion of Professor Copperud's expertise.

AN EXPERT ON ENGLISH LANGUAGE USAGE

Roy Copperud was a newspaper writer on major dailies for over three decades before embarking on a distinguished seventeen-year career teaching journalism at USC. Since 1952, Copperud has been writing a column dealing with the professional aspects of journalism for *Editor and Publisher*, a weekly magazine focusing on the journalism field.

He's on the usage panel of the *American Heritage Dictionary*, and *Merriam Webster's Usage Dictionary* frequently cites him as an expert. Copperud's fifth book on usage, *American Usage and Style: The Consensus*, has been in continuous print since 1981, and is the winner of the Association of American Publishers' Humanities Award.

That sounds like an expert to me.

After a brief telephone call to Professor Copperud in which I introduced myself but did not give him any indication of why I was interested, I sent the following letter:

"I am writing you to ask you for your professional opinion as an expert in English usage, to analyze the text of the Second Amendment to the United States Constitution, and extract the intent from the text.

"The text of the Second Amendment is, 'A well-regulated Militia, being necessary to the security of a free State, the right of the people to keep and bear Arms, shall not be infringed.'

"The debate over this amendment has been whether the first part of the sentence, 'A well-regulated Militia, being necessary to the security of a free State,' is a restrictive clause or a subordinate clause, with respect to the independent clause containing the subject of the sentence, 'the right of the people to keep and bear Arms, shall not be infringed.'

"I would request that your analysis of this sentence not take into consideration issues of political impact or public policy, but be restricted entirely to a linguistic analysis of its meaning and intent. Further, since your professional analysis will likely become part of litigation regarding the consequences of the Second Amendment, I ask that whatever analysis you make be a professional opinion that you would be willing to stand behind with your reputation, and even be willing to testify under oath to support, if necessary."

My letter framed several questions about the text of the Second Amendment, then concluded:

"I realize that I am asking you to take on a major responsibility and task with this letter. I am doing so because, as a citizen, I believe it is vitally important to extract the actual meaning of the Second Amendment. While I ask that your analysis not be affected by the political importance of its results, I ask that you do this because of that importance."

QUESTIONS AND ANSWERS

After several more letters and phone calls, in which we discussed terms for his doing such an analysis, but in which we never discussed either of our opinions regarding the Second Amendment, gun control, or any other political subject, Professor Copperud sent me the following analysis (into which I have italicized my questions for the sake of clarity):

The words "A well-regulated militia, being necessary to the security of a free state," contrary to the interpretation cited in your letter of July 26, 1991, constitutes a present participle, rather than a clause. It is used as an adjective, modifying "militia," which is followed by the main clause of the sentence (subject "the right," verb "shall"). The right to keep and bear arms is asserted as essential for maintaining a militia.

In reply to your numbered questions:

1) *Can the sentence be interpreted to grant the right to keep and bear arms solely to "a well-regulated militia"?*

The sentence does not restrict the right to keep and bear arms, nor does it state or imply possession of the right elsewhere or by others than the people; it simply makes a positive statement with respect to a right of the people.

2) *Is "the right of the people to keep and bear arms" granted by the words of the Second Amendment, or does the Second Amendment assume a pre-existing*

right of the people to keep and bear arms, and merely state that such right "shall not be infringed"?

The right is not granted by the amendment; its existence is assumed. The thrust of the sentence is that the right shall be preserved inviolate for the sake of ensuring a militia.

IS A MILITIA NECESSARY?

3) Is the right of the people to keep and bear arms conditioned upon whether or not a well-regulated militia, is, in fact, necessary to the security of a free State, and if that condition is not existing, is the statement "the right of the people to keep and bear Arms, shall not be infringed" null and void?

No such condition is expressed or implied. The right to keep and bear arms is not said by the amendment to depend on the existence of a militia. No condition is stated or implied as to the relation of the right to keep and bear arms and to the necessity of a well-regulated militia as a requisite to the security of a free state. The right to keep and bear arms is deemed unconditional by the entire sentence.

AN UNCONDITIONAL RIGHT

The meaning that the gun-controllers impose on the Second Amendment simply cannot be squared with the text. If the framers' concern had been to keep the national government from infringing on the state's freedom to form militias, they might have written: A well regulated militia being necessary for the security of a free state, the power of the states to form and control militias shall not be limited.

The main clause of that revision keeps the focus on states and militias, where the gun-controllers say it should be. In contrast, James Madison's main clause focuses on the people's right to keep and bear arms. How can it be reasonably concluded that the amendment means anything except that the people have an unconditional right to own and carry arms?

Sheldon Richman, *Human Events*, June 16, 1995.

---

4) Does the clause "A well-regulated Militia, being necessary to the security of a free State," grant a right to the government to place conditions on the "right of the people to keep and bear arms," or is such right deemed unconditional by the meaning of the entire sentence?

The right is assumed to exist and to be unconditional, as previously stated. It is invoked here specifically for the sake of the militia.

5) Which of the following does the phrase "well-regulated militia" mean:

"well-equipped," "well-organized," "well-drilled," "well-educated," or "subject to regulations of a superior authority"?

The phrase means "subject to regulations of a superior authority;" this accords with the desire of the writers for civilian control over the military.

6) If at all possible, I would ask you to take into account the changed meanings of words, or usage, since that sentence was written two hundred years ago, but not take into account historical interpretations of the intents of the authors, unless those issues cannot be clearly separated.

To the best of my knowledge, there has been no change in the meaning of words or in usage that would affect the meaning of the amendment. If it were written today, it might be put: "Since a well-regulated militia is necessary to the security of a free state, the right of the people to keep and bear arms shall not be abridged."

A "Scientific Control" for Language Usage

7) As a "scientific control" on this analysis, I would also appreciate it if you could compare your analysis of the text of the Second Amendment to the following sentence:

"A well-schooled electorate, being necessary to the security of a free State, the right of the people to keep and read Books, shall not be infringed."

My questions for the usage analysis of this sentence would be:

A) Is the grammatical structure and usage of this sentence and the way the words modify each other identical to the Second Amendment's sentence?

B) Could this sentence be interpreted to restrict "the right of the people to keep and read Books" only to "a well-educated electorate"—for example, registered voters with a high-school diploma?

A) Your "scientific control" sentence precisely parallels the amendment in grammatical structure.

B) There is nothing in your sentence that either indicates or implies the possibility of a restricted interpretation.

No Conclusion

Professor Copperud had only one additional comment, which he placed in his cover letter: "With well-known human curiosity, I made some speculative efforts to decide how the material might be used, but was unable to reach any conclusion."

So now we have been told by one of the top experts on American usage what many knew all along: the Constitution of the United States unconditionally protects the people's right to keep and bear arms, forbidding all governments formed under the Constitution from abridging that right. . . .

In the United States, elected lawmakers, judges, and appointed officials who are pledged to defend the Constitution of the United States ignore, marginalize, or prevaricate about the Second Amendment routinely. American citizens are put in American prisons for carrying arms, owning arms of forbidden sorts, or failing to satisfy bureaucratic requirements regarding the owning and carrying of firearms—all of which is an abridgement of the unconditional right of the people to keep and bear arms, guaranteed by the Constitution. Even the American Civil Liberties Union (ACLU), staunch defender of the rest of the Bill of Rights, stands by and does nothing.

It seems it is up to those who believe in the right to keep and bear arms to preserve that right. No one else will. No one else can. Will we beg our elected representatives not to take away our rights, and continue regarding them as representing us if they do? Will we continue obeying judges who decide that the Second Amendment doesn't mean what it says it means but means whatever they say it means in their Orwellian doublespeak?

Or will we simply keep and bear the arms of our choice, as the Constitution of the United States promises us we can, and pledge that we will defend that promise with our lives, our fortunes, and our sacred honor?

"Individual possession of handguns
may be banned completely without
offending the Second Amendment."

GUN CONTROL IS CONSTITUTIONAL

Chris Sprigman

In four separate cases, maintains Chris Sprigman in the following viewpoint, the Supreme Court has ruled that the right to
bear arms provided by the Second Amendment is not an absolute right. According to Sprigman, the Second Amendment is
designed to protect the right of state militias—not individual
citizens—to own firearms. Regulations against guns only become unconstitutional when privately owned guns are necessary for maintaining a militia, he contends. Since handguns are
unsuitable for use in a militia, Sprigman argues, laws controlling
private ownership of these weapons are constitutional. Sprigman is an attorney in New York City.

As you read, consider the following questions:

1. What was the Supreme Court's ruling in United States v. Miller, as
   cited by the author?
2. According to James Madison, as cited by Sprigman, what is
   the role of state militias?
3. According to the author, why are there fewer gun-related
   deaths in Canada, Japan, and Great Britain than in the United
   States?

Chris Sprigman, "This Is Not a Well-Regulated Militia," Open Forum, Winter 1994.
Reprinted by permission.

The American people increasingly favor gun control.

A December 1993 *Time/CNN* poll revealed that 92% of the public supported the Brady Bill, which imposes a 5-day waiting period on handgun purchases. The same poll showed that 60% of the public are in favor of even tougher measures.

But in spite of the public demand for tighter gun restrictions, the National Rifle Association and similar pro-gun organizations continue to oppose even such modest steps as the Brady Bill. Gun lobbyists believe, unhesitatingly and unyieldingly, that the Second Amendment to the U.S. Constitution grants the inalienable right to own guns, no matter the cost in lives.

But does the Second Amendment really guarantee an unrestricted right to possess deadly weaponry? The Supreme Court doesn't think so.

THE SUPREME COURT AND THE SECOND AMENDMENT

In *United States v. Miller* (1939), the Court upheld a federal law banning possession of sawed-off shotguns. The right to arms granted by the Second Amendment, the Court stated, is limited to weapons that bear a "reasonable relationship to the preservation or efficiency of a well-regulated militia." Possession of a sawed-off shotgun, which has no appreciable military use, could thus be banned.

The *Miller* Court based its holding directly on the Second Amendment's text, which provides that

> A well regulated Militia, being necessary to the security of a free State, the right of the people to keep and bear Arms, shall not be infringed.

As is clear from the text, the amendment's animating purpose is the maintenance of "well regulated" state militias. The Founders of this country relied upon state volunteer militias, organized and funded by the state governments, to provide a vital bulwark against possible tyranny from the new federal government and its standing army. James Madison, writing in *The Federalist Papers*, made clear the role of the state militias in maintaining a balance of power between the federal government and the states:

> Let a regular army, fully equal to the resources of the country, be formed; and let it be entirely at the devotion of the federal government; still it would not be going too far to say, that the State governments, with the people on their side, would be able to repel the danger.

The High Court's decision in *Miller*—and the three other times the Court considered the Second Amendment—honors the Founders' commitment to preserve the state militias, while making clear that the Second Amendment is not an absolute "right to bear arms."

Rather, the Second Amendment allows for the continuation of state militias and allows them to be effective by preventing federal confiscation of militia weapons—and that's *all* it does.

Private gun ownership that is not necessary to the maintenance of the militia is not protected by the Second Amendment.

THE SECOND AMENDMENT DOES NOT APPLY

The Supreme Court . . . in 1980 . . . reconfirmed that . . . "legislative restrictions on the use of firearms do not trench upon any constitutionally protected liberties.". . .

The legal precedents are clear: Almost any state or local gun-control action is fine; the Second Amendment does not apply. On the federal level, only laws interfering with state militias are prohibited.

Peter H. Stone, *Mother Jones*, January/February 1994.

Given the Second Amendment's narrow focus, there is simply no constitutional barrier to gun control measures. Handguns—which cause more death and injury on American streets than any other type of weapon—are mostly unsuitable for military use and are irrelevant to the maintenance of an effective militia. Under *Miller*, therefore, individual possession of handguns may be banned completely without offending the Second Amendment.

THE RIGHT OF PRIVATE GUN OWNERSHIP

When the Constitution and Bill of Rights were drafted, individual ownership of guns was necessary to the militia's smooth functioning—there was no other way to muster the militia with sufficient speed. The state militias of the 1800s, however, eventually became today's National Guard. And weapons of the National Guard are stored and distributed by the state and can be distributed quickly in emergencies.

Because individual gun ownership no longer has any relevance to maintaining an effective state militia, private citizens retain no Second Amendment right to bear arms. There is no constitutional barrier to wide-ranging, effective gun control.

That does not mean, however, that the Second Amendment is a dead letter. Should one or more states decide to reconstitute a volunteer militia, the Second Amendment guarantees that the state will be able to distribute arms to their citizen-soldiers in times of need, without federal interference.

This is the right to resist federal government tyranny that the Founders were eager to enshrine in the Bill of Rights. What they did not intend to enshrine is the right for any person to obtain any sort of firearm with little obstacle.

GUN VIOLENCE ABROAD

In this country, 40,000 people were killed by guns in 1993. Each day, 111 more people die by gunfire. The NRA and other gun advocates claim that gun control can't work. Yet, in the same murderous year that the U.S. has just passed through [1993], far fewer gun deaths occurred abroad: 76 people were shot to death in Canada, 82 in Japan, and only 33 in Great Britain. In fact, there were fewer gun-related deaths in all three of those countries combined than in an average mid-sized American city.

And the violence doesn't end there. Gunfire caused serious injuries to over 100,000 Americans in 1993, and guns were used to commit over 600,000 nonlethal rapes, robberies, kidnappings, burglaries and carjackings. All of these figures are dramatically lower in every other industrial nation.

Part of the difference, of course, is that other countries have had the sense to limit easy access to guns. Their constitutions do not prevent rational, effective gun control.

And, thankfully, neither does ours.

PERIODICAL BIBLIOGRAPHY

The following articles have been selected to supplement the diverse views presented in this chapter. Addresses are provided for periodicals not indexed in the *Readers' Guide to Periodical Literature*, the *Alternative Press Index*, the *Social Sciences Index*, or the *Index to Legal Periodicals and Books*.

Joan Biskupic   "A Second (Amendment) Look at Bearing Arms," *Washington Post National Weekly Edition*, May 15–21, 1995.

Richard Cohen   "The NRA's Misinterpretation of Second Amendment," *Liberal Opinion Week*, May 29, 1995. Available from PO Box 468, Vinton, IA 52349-0468.

Stephen P. Halbrook   "The Right of the People or the Power of the State: Bearing Arms, Arming Militias, and the Second Amendment," *Journal on Firearms and Public Policy*, Fall 1994. Available from 12500 NE Tenth Pl., Bellevue, WA 98005.

Andrea Sachs   "Why the Second Amendment Is a Loser in Court," *Time*, May 29, 1995.

Chi Chi Sileo   "Gun Control War Targets Our Worst Nightmares," *Insight*, June 6, 1994. Available from 3600 New York Ave. NE, Washington, DC 20002.

Jacob Sullum   "Shooting Gallery," *Reason*, December 1995.

Tennessee Law Review   Second Amendment Symposium, Spring 1995.

William Van Alstyne   "The Second Amendment and the Personal Right to Arms," *Journal on Firearms and Public Policy*, Fall 1995.

Garry Wills   "To Keep and Bear Arms," *New York Review of Books*, September 21, 1995.

William Winter   "The Founding Fathers' Bill of Rights," *Human Quest*, July/August 1995. Available from 1074 23rd Ave. N., St. Petersburg, FL 33704.

Gordon Witkin et al.   "The Fight to Bear Arms," *U.S. News & World Report*, May 22, 1995.

Richard L. Worsnop   "Gun Control," *CQ Researcher*, June 10, 1994.

CHAPTER 3

IS GUN OWNERSHIP AN EFFECTIVE MEANS OF SELF-DEFENSE?

CHAPTER PREFACE

A gang of four masked thieves broke into Marsha Beatty's home in Fort Wayne, Indiana, in December 1995, only to be confronted by Beatty with her 9-mm pistol. When one thief hesitated after being told to drop his TEC-9 semiautomatic pistol, Beatty threatened to kill him. The thief and his three companions then fled, while Beatty and her roommate, who also had a 9-mm handgun, pursued them. "When they saw two women with guns, they ran," Beatty said.

Susan White-Bowden of Finksburg, Maryland, grew up with guns in the house and was comfortable around them. Even after her former husband committed suicide with one of her guns in 1974, she did not remove them from her home. But two and a half years later, her seventeen-year-old son—who was having problems with his girlfriend—took one of his mother's handguns and killed himself. There are no longer any guns in White-Bowden's house. "I would be killed at the hand of a robber six times over before I would allow any guns near any of [my six grandchildren]," she told the Senate Judiciary Committee in a 1995 hearing about guns and self-defense.

Gun-control opponents and supporters argue whether guns are necessary for self-protection or whether they are too dangerous to be used for protection. Approximately thirty-eight thousand to forty thousand people are killed in the United States in gun-related accidents, suicides, and homicides every year. Gun-control advocates believe that the number of gun-related deaths is unacceptably high. They cite a study by Arthur Kellerman, a doctor and researcher, that found that a gun in a home is forty-three times more likely to be used to kill a member of the household than to be used in self-defense. Opponents of gun control maintain, however, that a study by researcher Gary Kleck shows that guns are used in self-defense over two million times a year. His study also estimates that about four hundred thousand people a year use their guns in situations where they believe that doing so "definitely saved a life." Kleck contends, "If even one-tenth of these people are accurate in their stated perception, the number of lives saved by victim use of guns would still exceed the total number of lives taken with guns."

In the controversy over gun control, one of the most debated issues is that of the use of guns for self-defense. In the following chapter, researchers and others examine the costs and benefits of using guns for self-defense.

| "The Justice Department's statistics show that if you're attacked, your best chance of getting away unhurt is to pull a gun."

GUNS ARE AN EFFECTIVE MEANS OF SELF-DEFENSE

Joel Rosenberg

In the following viewpoint, Joel Rosenberg recounts how his home was burglarized one night while his family slept. He maintains that he frightened the thieves off by threatening to use his gun. Rosenberg contends that he and his family may have been seriously injured by the armed burglars if he had not had a gun. Guns, he argues, provide an effective means of self-defense for families and homeowners. Rosenberg is a science fiction and fantasy writer in Minneapolis, Minnesota.

As you read, consider the following questions:

1. According to the author, what did the burglars take from the Rosenberg home?
2. How many Americans defend themselves with handguns, according to Rosenberg?
3. According to the author, how do citizens who have carry permits for their handguns affect crime?

Adapted from "Protecting Home and Hearth with Guns" by Joel Rosenberg, Minneapolis-St. Paul Star-Tribune, January 23, 1994. Reprinted with the author's permission.

On July 15th, 1990—five days after my daughter's first birthday—at just about four in the morning, the burglar in our bedroom reached a hand under the covers, on my wife's side.

Felicia came awake instantly and shouted, "There's somebody in the room!" I snapped awake and shot out of bed, shouting—bellowing, Felicia says—something to the effect of how I was going to get my gun and kill the bastard.

I think the burglar was already fleeing when I yanked open the drawer. I remember thinking, as I pulled out my then newly-acquired 9mm Ruger P-85—yes, the same model that Colin Ferguson used to kill a bunch of unarmed commuters in 1993—that I had to get a good view of him before I shot him, because our daughter was across the hall in her room, and for all I knew, he was holding her. And I remember thinking that if he was holding her, I'd have to shoot low and hit him in the legs, or high, and shoot him in the head.

Or both.

F FOR FIRE

But we had a trigger lock on the Ruger, and in the dark I couldn't find my keys, so I ran to the bureau and ripped open the locked bag with the .22 target pistol in it, fumbled in the dark until I found its magazine (a politically incorrect 13-round magazine, by the way) and slammed it into the pistol, racking the slide as I ran to check on Judy—who, thankfully, slept through the whole thing.

I remember thinking that the slide had worked too easily, so I wasted a round by racking it again, dumping a cartridge on the carpet, and then I carefully pushed the safety switch off, toward that little F for Fire—and took a deep breath.

He was gone. My wife and daughter were safe, and they were behind me, and there was no sense in gambling, chasing a burglar or burglars off into the night.

So I just crouched at the top of the stairs—looking nothing at all like Mel Gibson or Arnold Schwarzenegger—in my jockey shorts with the potbelly hanging over the waistband in front, thinking that if one of them came up the stairs I'd put three rounds in his chest, and one in his head. (Actually, I distinctly remember thinking, "I'll put three warning shots in his chest, and one warning shot in his head." It didn't seem funny then.)

And I also remember reminding myself not to put my finger on the trigger until I had a target to shoot at, and I never did end up putting my finger on the trigger that morning, because they had all run away, and when the police arrived—I'm told it was less than five minutes; it felt like a couple of years—we were dressed, and went downstairs to look at the damage.

At least three of them, probably four—it would take at least two people to lift our large-sized TV set, and it looked like one of them was working on the VCR and another was emptying out Felicia's purse while the third came upstairs. There's some reason to believe it was the gang known as the Nokomis Bandits, whom we read about a few days later, a gang of four who had steadily ratcheted up their level of violence; if so, we got off a lot easier than most of their victims.

A Distinctive Sound

There was an intrusion. . . .

I woke up as the assailants broke in and I calmly walked to our closet where the firearm was stored. I grabbed my Colt AR-15 semiautomatic rifle chambered in .223 Remington. I inserted the magazine while I was in the closet. I walked to the top of the stairs. Then I pulled back the bolt, and, letting it go, chambered a round.

That distinctive sound—indeed, that sound and the distinctive appearance of this firearm—was all I needed to protect four innocent lives and send multiple perpetrators scurrying.

As in most self-defense uses of guns, no shot was fired.

Sharon-Jo Ramboz, statement before the U.S. House of Representatives Judiciary Committee's Subcommittee on Crime, March 31, 1995.

As such things go, it wasn't all that bad.

They got: Felicia's Banana Republic bag; her credit cards and wallet, containing about $30 cash; about $20 in a container of quarters we keep—kept—for change; our huge Sharp TV set; my answering machine; her keys and ID; a TV cable; my business card case; a few other odds and ends.

And they took our sense of security. Our home didn't seem to be the safe place it was before.

Oh—and they got another thing, something I only noticed a couple of days later, when I went to carve a roast: they took a butcher knife from the kitchen.

I sat down and shook for a few minutes. And I didn't mention it to Felicia for a number of months. A butcher knife.

Neither Felicia nor I slept through the night for many months, and even now I wake quickly at the slightest sound.

I'm not a violent guy, honest. In fifteen years together, certainly including the occasional loud argument like most couples have, I've never so much as raised my hand to my wife, and I save spanking my daughter for important issues like, say, running into the street or playing with the burners on the stove (and even then, I don't hit her hard; I hate hitting kids). That's no big deal; that's all pretty ordinary.

All of it's very ordinary, really. And what happened to us wasn't unusual—upwards of a million Americans every year defend themselves with handguns, and in the vast majority of cases, no shot is fired. Not surprising—the Justice Department's statistics show that if you're attacked, your best chance of getting away unhurt is to pull a gun. In the states where law-abiding citizens can easily get carry permits, like Florida, and Oregon, and our neighboring state of South Dakota, nobody can seem to find cases of permit-carrying citizens committing gun crimes, although there are many accounts of legally armed citizens stopping crimes.

Every time I hear the latest cry to take handguns away from ordinary citizens (and, of course, those few criminals who are willing to obey such laws), I think about the night we lucked out, and how glad I am that such laws weren't in force that night.

And I wonder—I'll never know—what he and his friends would have done if instead of bellowing, "I'm getting my gun and killing the bastard?" I'd said, "Please don't hurt us, please?"

Fled anyway? (And where was that butcher knife?)

Maybe.

No Apology

We made some changes since the burglary: we added a security system, and prominently display the signs and decals, hoping that the next burglar will just go on to another house.

And, just in case he doesn't, we keep a loaded gun in a push-button-locked gun box just over the bed. And we keep it without apology.

| "A gun is not a particularly good defense strategy, especially where there are small children in the home."

GUNS ARE NOT AN EFFECTIVE MEANS OF SELF-DEFENSE

Barbara L. Keller

Despite experiencing a late-night break-in, Barbara L. Keller maintains in the following viewpoint that guns are not a good means of self-protection. Keeping loaded guns around children is dangerous, she contends, and unloaded guns are not effective for self-defense. In addition, Keller argues, a person who brandishes a gun in self-defense actually increases the potential that he or she will be harmed in a violent confrontation. Keller is a lawyer who writes on legal and medical issues.

As you read, consider the following questions:

1. What is the result of the lack of gun-control legislation, according to the author?
2. In the author's opinion, what are society's three options for dealing with crime and criminals?
3. Who should have the right to bear arms, according to Keller?

Barbara L. Keller, "Frontiersmen Are History," *Newsweek*, August 16, 1993. Copyright ©1993 by Newsweek, Inc. All rights reserved. Reprinted by permission.

L ate on a Friday night, I had a personal introduction to terror. My 11-year-old daughter and I were playing Scrabble. My husband had just phoned to let us know he was grounded in Dallas by bad weather. A moment later my front doorbell rang loudly and repeatedly. I stood up, wondering who in God's name was ringing at 1 o'clock in the morning. Then I heard the sound of shattering glass. Someone was breaking into my house.

As I grabbed my daughter and dashed out the side door to my neighbor's to call the police, she began to cry. "Mom! What about the boys?" My three sons—3, 4 and a mentally handicapped 8-year-old—were asleep upstairs. I had made a split-second decision to leave them and run for help. To go to them, or the phone, would have taken me right into harm's way. Being eight months pregnant, I couldn't carry them two at a time to safety. The minutes it took until the police arrived seemed like years. I wasn't permitted to enter the house until the officers had secured it. I stood on the sidewalk, fearing for my sons' safety and worrying about their reaction if they awoke to find armed policemen trooping through their bedroom. Blessedly, the boys slept through it, and the would-be intruders ran off without entering the house.

Not a Good Defense

In the aftermath of what was for me a horribly traumatic experience, my husband and I considered and once again rejected the idea of buying a gun for protection. Police officers have told me a gun is not a particularly good defense strategy, especially where there are small children in the home. If the gun isn't loaded—or the ammunition isn't very nearby—it's not likely to be much help in a situation needing a fast reaction. Yet if it is loaded and handy, it poses a serious threat to children—and others.

Like most residents of Baton Rouge, I have strong views on gun control. Unlike most, I am for it. You have to understand that this is Louisiana. We have been characterized humorously, but I fear accurately, as a society of good ole boys who consider the shotguns displayed in the back of the pickup as a God-given right and a status symbol. We don't much care for being told what to do, especially by the government. During the trial of Rodney Peairs, acquitted of killing a Japanese exchange student who he mistakenly thought was invading his home on Halloween in 1992, a local news program conducted a telephone poll on the question of gun control. At that time, 68 percent of the respondents opposed stricter controls. Such measures routinely fail in our legislature, as they do in Congress.

One result is that we have criminals armed with semiautomatic and assault weapons and a police force that is seriously outgunned. Our options, as I see them, are three: maintain the status quo, make it more difficult for criminals to obtain these weapons, or provide them to the police as well. The status quo is to me unacceptable, and the notion of a police force armed with assault rifles roaming the streets of Baton Rouge does not bring solace to my soul. It terrifies me. That leaves the option of gun control.

Why does this prospect engender such hysteria? I do not propose to outlaw guns—only to make them more difficult to obtain. No one with a criminal record or history of violent mental illness—and no child—should by law be able to purchase a gun. And no one has a compelling need to buy an assault weapon.

TEMPTING FATE

None of this may make a hill of beans of difference, directly, in the case of a homeowner protecting himself from real or perceived threats. But indirectly it can. We should rethink our cultural heritage and the historical gunslinger's mentality of "a Smith & Wesson beats four aces." We've outgrown the frontier spirit and the need of weapons for survival. In Baton Rouge, I am a definite oddity in not allowing my children, including my normal, rambunctious little boys, to play at shooting people. I don't want my children to think of guns as problem solvers. Nor do I favor the simplistic depictions of good guys versus bad guys.

IMAGINATION VS. REALITY

People imagine themselves getting the drop on the bad guy, confronting the craven coward in mid-swagger. They will make the villains run in fear from an armed and righteous citizenry, and order will again prevail. . . .

In fact, they will first see another's gun when its barrel is pointed straight at them, their own gun undrawable even if it were reachable. Or maybe their gun will be stolen, which just about guarantees it will become a murder weapon.

Luc Sante, New York Times, December 9, 1993.

What really frightens me is that if I were faced with the prospect of imminent harm to myself or my children and had a gun at the ready, I would reach for it, despite my feelings against using firearms for personal protection. Panic is a compelling emotion and basically incompatible with reason. It is tempting fate severely to keep a powerful weapon available to deal with panic-inducing circumstances. The police are trained in when and how to shoot, and innocent people can still fall victim to an officer's adrenaline surge.

I will for a very long time remember the sound of glass breaking and feel all over again the fear mingled with disbelief of that Friday night. If I'd owned a gun, I undoubtedly would have used it—probably to my own detriment. I do not know if the young men who so thoroughly violated my sense of safety were armed. I do know that if I'd had a gun, and had actually confronted them, they would have been more likely to harm me, and my children. It would have been I who escalated the potential for violence, and I would have had to live with the consequences—just like Rodney Peairs.

RECONSIDERING AMERICA'S LOVE AFFAIR

Although I have felt the terror of helplessness, owning a handgun is something I cannot do. And the "Shoot first, ask questions later" approach is an attitude I don't want to teach my children. Guns are like cars. We are so inured to their power we tend to treat them irresponsibly. We see them as commodities that we have a right to own and use as we please. Instead, we should limit the "right to bear arms" so that only trained, responsible citizens can buy guns for sport, recreation and protection—while those who would be most likely to use weapons detrimentally will have a much harder time getting them. Most of all, we need to reconsider our entire love affair with guns and the ways that this passion destroys innocent lives.

"Each year in the U.S. there are about 2.2 to 2.5 million [defensive gun uses] of all types by civilians."

DEFENSIVE GUN USE IS COMMON

Gary Kleck and Marc Gertz

Gary Kleck and Marc Gertz contend in the following viewpoint that defensive gun use (DGU) is much more common than a widely quoted survey by the federal government indicates. Kleck and Gertz argue that the government survey's results are inaccurate because people are afraid to tell government researchers the truth about their possibly illegal use of guns to defend themselves against criminals. The results of their anonymous survey are far more accurate, the authors maintain. Moreover, they assert, other studies support their findings of over 2 million DGUs per year. Kleck is a professor of criminology and criminal justice at Florida State University and the author of several studies on the use of firearms for defensive purposes. Gertz is an associate professor of criminology and criminal justice at Florida State University.

As you read, consider the following questions:
1. How many instances of defensive gun use are reported by the National Crime Victimization Survey (NCVS), as cited by the authors?
2. What was the National Crime Victimization Survey designed for, in the authors' opinion?
3. According to Kleck and Gertz, how did they ensure that their survey on defensive gun use produced more accurate results than the NCVS?

Excerpted from Gary Kleck and Marc Gertz, "Armed Resistance to Crime: The Prevalence and Nature of Self-Defense with a Gun." Reprinted by special permission of Northwestern University School of Law from Journal of Criminal Law and Criminology, vol. 86, no. 1, pp. 153-57, 160, 167-69, 180-81, 184 (1995).

H owever consistent the evidence may be concerning the effectiveness of armed victim resistance, there are some who minimize its significance by insisting that it is rare. This assertion is invariably based entirely on a single source of information, the National Crime Victimization Survey (NCVS).

INCONSISTENT ESTIMATES

Data from the NCVS imply that each year there are only about 68,000 defensive uses of guns in connection with assaults and robberies, or about 80,000 to 82,000 if one adds in uses linked with household burglaries. These figures are less than one-ninth of the estimates implied by the results of at least thirteen other surveys, most of which have been previously reported. The NCVS estimates imply that about 0.09 of 1% of U.S. households experience a defensive gun use (DGU) in any one year, compared to the Mauser survey's estimate of 3.79% of households over a five year period, or about 0.76% in any one year, assuming an even distribution over the five year period, and no repeat uses.

The strongest evidence that a measurement is inaccurate is that it is inconsistent with many other independent measurements or observations of the same phenomenon; indeed, some would argue that this is ultimately the only way of knowing that a measurement is wrong. Therefore, one might suppose that the gross inconsistency of the NCVS-based estimates with all other known estimates, each derived from sources with no known flaws even remotely substantial enough to account for nine-to-one, or more, discrepancies, would be sufficient to persuade any serious scholar that the NCVS estimates are unreliable. . . .

LIMITATIONS OF THE NCVS SURVEY

Equally important, those who take the NCVS-based estimates seriously have consistently ignored the most pronounced limitations of the NCVS for estimating DGU frequency. The NCVS is a non-anonymous national survey conducted by a branch of the federal government, the U.S. Bureau of the Census. Interviewers identify themselves to Rs [respondents] as federal government employees, even displaying, in face-to-face contacts, an identification card with a badge. Rs are told that the interviews are being conducted on behalf of the U.S. Department of Justice, the law enforcement branch of the federal government. As a preliminary to asking questions about crime victimization experiences, interviewers establish the address, telephone number, and full names of all occupants, age twelve and over, in each household they contact. In short, it is made very clear to Rs that they are, in effect, speaking to a law enforcement arm of the federal government, whose employees know exactly who the Rs and their family members are, where they live, and how they can be recontacted.

Even under the best of circumstances, reporting the use of a gun for self-protection would be an extremely sensitive and legally controversial matter for either of two reasons. As with other forms of forceful resistance, the defensive act itself, regardless of the characteristics of any weapon used, might constitute an unlawful assault or at least the R might believe that others, including either legal authorities or the researchers, could regard it that way. Resistance with a gun also involves additional elements of sensitivity. Because guns are legally regulated, a victim's possession of the weapon, either in general or at the time of the DGU, might itself be unlawful, either in fact or in the mind of a crime victim who used one. More likely, lay persons with a limited knowledge of the extremely complicated law of either self-defense or firearms regulation are unlikely to know for sure whether their defensive actions or their gun possession was lawful.

EASY TO WITHHOLD INFORMATION

It is not hard for gun-using victims interviewed in the NCVS to withhold information about their use of a gun, especially since they are *never directly asked whether they used a gun for self-protection*. They are asked only general questions about whether they did anything to protect themselves. In short, Rs are merely given the opportunity to volunteer the information that they have used a gun defensively. All it takes for an R to conceal a DGU is to simply refrain from mentioning it, i.e., to leave it out of what may be an otherwise accurate and complete account of the crime incident.

Further, Rs in the NCVS are not even asked the general self-protection question unless they already independently indicated that they had been a victim of a crime. This means that any DGUs associated with crimes the Rs did not want to talk about would remain hidden. It has been estimated that the NCVS may catch less than one-twelfth of spousal assaults and one-thirty-third of rapes, thereby missing nearly all DGUs associated with such crimes. . . .

THE SURVEY'S PURPOSE

The NCVS was not designed to estimate how often people resist crime using a gun. It was designed primarily to estimate national victimization levels; it incidentally happens to include a few self-protection questions which include response categories covering resistance with a gun. Its survey instrument has been carefully refined and evaluated over the years to do as good a job as possible in getting people to report illegal things which other people have done to them. This is the exact opposite of the task which faces anyone trying to get good DGU estimates—to get people to admit controversial and possibly illegal things which the Rs themselves have done. Therefore, it is neither surprising, nor a reflection on the survey's designers, to note that the NCVS is singularly ill-suited for estimating the prevalence or incidence of DGU. It is not credible to regard this survey as an acceptable basis for establishing, in even the roughest way, how often Americans use guns for self-protection. . . .

THE NATIONAL SELF-DEFENSE SURVEY

The present survey is the first survey ever devoted to the subject of armed self-defense. It was carefully designed to correct all of the known correctable or avoidable flaws of previous surveys which critics have identified. We use the most anonymous possible national survey format, the anonymous random digit dialed telephone survey. We did not know the identities of those who were interviewed, and made this fact clear to the Rs. We interviewed a large nationally representative sample covering all adults, age eighteen and over, in the lower forty-eight states and living in households with telephones. We asked DGU questions of all Rs in our sample, asking them separately about both their own DGU experiences and those of other members of their households. We used both a five year recall period and a one year recall period. We inquired about uses of both handguns and other types of guns and excluded occupational uses of guns and uses against animals. Finally, we asked a long series of detailed questions designed to establish exactly what Rs did with their guns; for example, if they had confronted other humans, and how had each DGU connected to a specific crime or crimes. . . .

Questions about the details of DGU incidents permitted us to establish whether a given DGU met all of the following qualifications for an incident to be treated as a genuine DGU: (1) the incident involved defensive action against a human rather than an animal, but not in connection with police, military, or security guard duties; (2) the incident involved actual contact with a person, rather than merely investigating suspicious circumstances, etc.; (3) the defender could state a specific crime which he thought was being committed at the time of the incident; (4) the gun was actually used in some way—at a minimum it had to be used as part of a threat against a person, either by verbally referring to the gun (e.g., "get away—I've got a gun") or by pointing it at an adversary. We made no effort to assess either the lawfulness or morality of the Rs' defensive actions. . . .

DEFENSIVE GUN USAGE

The most technically sound estimates presented in Table 1 are those based on the shorter one year recall period that rely on Rs' firsthand accounts of their own experiences (person-based estimates). These estimates appear in the first two columns. They indicate that each year in the U.S. there are about 2.2 to 2.5 million DGUs of all types by civilians against humans, with about 1.5 to 1.9 million of the incidents involving use of handguns.

These estimates are larger than those derived from the best

TABLE 1. CIVILIAN DEFENSIVE GUN USE, U.S., 1988–1993[1]

Recall Period:		Past Year			
Base:		Person		Household	
Gun Types:		All Guns	Handguns	All Guns	Handguns
Persons/	A:[2]	2,549,862	1,893,079	1,540,405	1,072,434
Households	B:[2]	2,163,519	1,545,371	1,325,918	896,945
Annual Uses	A:	2,549,862	1,893,079	1,540,405	1,072,434
	B:	2,163,519	1,545,371	1,325,918	896,945

Recall Period:		Past Five Years			
Base:		Person		Household	
Gun Types:		All Guns	Handguns	All Guns	Handguns
Persons/	A:[2]	6,374,655	5,099,724	3,782,767	2,885,822
Households	B:[2]	5,717,872	4,442,941	3,353,794	2,515,345
Annual Uses	A:	1,884,348	1,442,941	1,158,283	515,345
	B:	1,683,342	888,588	1,029,615	505,069

Notes:

1. Defensive uses of guns against humans by civilians (i.e., excluding uses by police officers, security guards, or military personnel).

2. A estimates are based on all reported defensive gun uses reported in the survey; B estimates are based on only cases with no indications that the case might not be a genuine defensive gun use.

Population Bases: Estimated resident population, age eighteen and over, U.S., April, 1993: 190,538,000; estimated households (assuming the 1992–1993 percentage increase was the same as the 1991–1992 increase): 97,045,525 (U.S. Bureau of the Census, 1993, at 17, 55).

Gary Kleck and Marc Gertz, Journal of Criminal Law and Criminology, Fall 1995.

previous surveys, indicating that technical improvements in the measurement procedures have . . . *increased* rather than decreased estimates of the frequency that DGUs occur. Defensive gun use is thus just another specific example of a commonplace pattern in criminological survey work, which includes victimization surveys, self-report surveys of delinquency, surveys of illicit drug use, etc.: the better the measurement procedures, the higher the estimates of controversial behaviors. . . .

PLAUSIBLE ESTIMATES

Are these estimates plausible? Could it really be true that Americans use guns for self-protection as often as 2.1 to 2.5 million times a year? The estimate may seem remarkable in comparison to expectations based on conventional wisdom, but it is not implausibly large in comparison to various gun-related phenomena. There are probably over 220 million guns in private hands in the U.S., implying that only about 1% of them are used for defensive purposes in any one year—not an impossibly high fraction. In a December 1993 Gallup survey, 49% of U.S. households reported owning a gun, and 31% of adults reported personally owning one. These figures indicate that there are about 47.6 million households with a gun, with perhaps 93 million, or 49% of the adult U.S. population, living in households with guns, and about 59.1 million adults personally owning a gun. Again, it hardly seems implausible that 3% (2.5 million/93 million) of the people with immediate access to a gun could have used one defensively in a given year.

Huge numbers of Americans not only have access to guns, but the overwhelming majority of gun owners, if one can believe their statements, are willing to use a gun defensively. In a December 1989 national survey, 78% of American gun owners stated that they would not only be willing to use a gun defensively in some way, but would be willing to *shoot* a burglar. The percentage willing to use a gun defensively in *some* way, though not necessarily by shooting someone, would presumably be even higher than this.

Nevertheless, having access to a gun and being willing to use it against criminals is not the same as actually doing so. The latter requires experiencing a crime under circumstances in which the victim can get to, or already possesses, a gun. We do not know how many such opportunities for crime victims to use guns defensively occur each year. It would be useful to know how large a fraction of crimes with direct offender-victim contact result in a DGU. Unfortunately, a large share of the incidents covered by our survey are probably outside the scope of incidents that realistically are likely to be reported to either the NCVS or police. If the DGU incidents reported in the present survey are not entirely a subset within the pool of cases covered by the NCVS, one cannot meaningfully use NCVS data to estimate the share of crime incidents which result in a DGU. Nevertheless, in a ten state sample of incarcerated felons interviewed in 1982, 34% reported having been "scared off, shot at, wounded or captured by an armed victim." From the criminals' standpoint, this experience was not rare.

AN INVISIBLE PHENOMENON

How could such a serious thing happen so often without becoming common knowledge? This phenomenon, regardless of how widespread it really is, is largely an invisible one as far as governmental statistics are concerned. Neither the defender/victim nor the criminal ordinarily has much incentive to report this sort of event to the police, and either or both often have strong reasons not to do so. Consequently, many of these incidents never come to the attention of the police, while others may be reported but without victims' mentioning their use of a gun. And even when a DGU is reported, it will not necessarily be recorded by the police, who ordinarily do not keep statistics on matters other than DGUs resulting in a death, since police record-keeping is largely confined to information helpful in apprehending perpetrators and making a legal case for convicting them. Because such statistics are not kept, we cannot even be certain that a large number of DGUs are not reported to the police.

The health system cannot shed much light on this phenomenon either, since very few of these incidents involve injuries. In the rare case where someone is hurt, it is usually the criminal, who is unlikely to seek medical attention for any but the most life-threatening gunshot wounds, as this would ordinarily result in a police interrogation. Physicians in many states are required by law to report treatment of gunshot wounds to the police, making it necessary for medically treated criminals to explain to police how they received their wounds.

MOST DGUs ARE NOT REPORTED

Finally, it is now clear that virtually none of the victims who use guns defensively tell interviewers about it in the NCVS. Our estimates imply that only about 3% of DGUs among NCVS Rs are reported to interviewers. Based on other comparisons of alternative survey estimates of violent events with NCVS estimates, this high level of underreporting is eminently plausible. Colin Loftin and Ellen J. Mackenzie reported that rapes might be thirty-three times as frequent as NCVS estimates indicate, while spousal violence could easily be twelve times as high.

There is no inherent value to knowing the exact number of DGUs any more than there is any value to knowing the exact number of crimes which are committed each year. The estimates in Table 1 are at best only rough approximations, which are probably too low. It is sufficient to conclude from these numbers that DGU is very common, far more common than has been recognized to date by criminologists or policy makers, and certainly far more common than one would think based on any official sources of information. . . .

Valid and Invalid Estimates

There is little legitimate reason to continue accepting the NCVS estimates of DGU frequency as even approximately valid. The gross inconsistencies between the NCVS and all other sources of information make it reasonable to suppose that all but a handful of NCVS victims who had used a gun for protection in the reported incidents refrained from mentioning this gun use. In light of evidence on the injury-preventing effectiveness of victim gun use, in some cases where the absence of victim injury is credited to either nonresistance or some unarmed form of resistance, the absence of injury may have actually been due to resistance with a gun, which the victim failed to mention to the interviewer. . . .

Since as many as 400,000 people a year use guns in situations where the defenders claim that they "almost certainly" saved a life by doing so, this result cannot be dismissed as trivial. If even one-tenth of these people are accurate in their stated perceptions, the number of lives saved by victim use of guns would still exceed the total number of lives taken with guns. It is not possible to know how many lives are actually saved this way, for the simple reason that no one can be certain how crime incidents would have turned out had the participants acted differently than they actually did. But surely this is too serious a matter to simply assume that practically everyone who says he believes he saved a life by using a gun was wrong.

This is also too serious a matter to base conclusions on silly statistics comparing the number of lives taken with guns with the number of criminals killed by victims. Killing a criminal is not a benefit to the victim, but rather a nightmare to be suffered for years afterward. Saving a life through DGU would be a benefit, but this almost never involves killing the criminal; probably fewer than 3,000 criminals are lawfully killed by gun-wielding victims each year, representing only about $\frac{1}{1000}$ of the number of DGUs, and less than 1% of the number of purportedly life-saving DGUs. Therefore, the number of justifiable homicides cannot serve as even a rough index of life-saving gun uses. Since this comparison does not involve any measured benefit, it can shed no light on the benefits and costs of keeping guns in the home for protection.

"Approximately 82,000 persons use firearms each year in defense of person or property."

Defensive Gun Use Is Not Common

Garen J. Wintemute

In the following viewpoint, Garen J. Wintemute argues that the use of guns as protection against crime is not as common as reported in some studies. Surveys that report high levels of defensive gun use (DGU) are flawed, he maintains, especially because they are polled from extremely small samples and include questions that are open to interpretation. Wintemute also contends that keeping a gun for defensive use greatly increases the likelihood that the weapon will be used to injure or kill the gunowner or other family members. Wintemute is the director of the Violence Prevention Research Program at the University of California at Davis.

As you read, consider the following questions:

1. What size was the polled sample in the National Crime Victimization Survey, as cited by the author?
2. How large were Gary Kleck's samples in his polls on defensive gun use, according to Wintemute?
3. How many violent crimes involve handguns each year, according to the author?

From Garen J. Wintemute's testimony before the Senate Judiciary Committee, Subcommittee on Crime, March 31, 1995.

Today, nearly two-thirds (62%) of Americans describe themselves as "truly desperate" about crime and their personal safety. In that desperation, almost two-thirds (62%) of Americans feel that the need to have a gun for personal protection is increasing. Yet at the same time, an essentially identical 61% of Americans feel that the ready availability of guns has contributed "a great deal" to rates of violence. And less than half of gun owners believe that having a gun makes them safer from crime.

Herein lies the difficult question that is at the heart of the matter we are discussing today: Is ready availability of guns at home and on the street part of the problem, part of the solution, or both?

PART OF THE PROBLEM

We have come generally to recognize that, for at least some parts of our population, the use of firearms for protection is part of the problem. For example, few Americans would consider it a positive phenomenon that, as determined by criminologist James Wright and colleagues, 22% of inner-city high school students have guns and 35% of students usually or sometimes carry guns.

These students overwhelmingly cite the need for protection as their motivation for gun carrying. Their concerns are real. Nearly half the students in Professor Wright's survey (45%) had been threatened with a gun or shot at on the way to or from school in recent years; a question including incidents at other times during the day would have undoubtedly yielded higher figures. In another study of inner-city students, those who had been threatened or attacked with a gun were more than 3 times as likely as others to carry a gun for protection.

Studies of the general population of gun owners report that guns are frequently kept easily accessible for defensive use. More than half of gun owners have at least one gun stored loaded, and more than half keep one or more guns not locked up; at least 20% report keeping a loaded gun readily available and not locked away. Gun carrying is also widespread. In one national survey of gun owners, nearly half (42%) of the 369 persons who reported handgun ownership stated that they carried their handgun with them at least occasionally.

DEFENSIVE GUN USE

One key question is: How often are guns used for legitimate defensive purposes? There are many instances each year in which people make defensive use of firearms in ways that all of us would consider to be beneficial. But estimates of the number of times this occurs vary widely.

The best source of such information is the National Crime Victimization Survey, conducted by the Bureau of the Census for the Bureau of Justice Statistics. It is a sample of 59,000 housing units in the United States. Making use of these data, researchers estimate that during the years 1987–1992 there were on average 62,200 persons who used firearms to defend themselves. About 20% of these were law enforcement officers acting in the line of duty, reducing the annual estimate of the civilian defensive use of firearms to about 50,000 cases per year. Another 20,300 persons each year used a firearm to defend their property from theft.

GARY KLECK'S ESTIMATES

A much higher and widely quoted estimate, in the neighborhood of 1 million instances of defensive use per year, was generated by Gary Kleck of Florida State University. The size of the discrepancy makes it important to consider its sources. Professor Kleck made use of data from a public opinion poll of less than 1,300 registered voters who were asked the following question: "Within the past five years, have you, yourself, or another member of your household used a handgun, even if it was not fired, for self-protection or for the protection of property at home, work, or elsewhere, excluding military service and police security work?" Four percent of respondents (49 persons) responded "yes" to this question. The Kleck estimate is believed to have two significant flaws. First, the general nature of the question does not exclude such uses of a firearm as carrying it in one's car or in one's pocket as protective use. A more proper question would restrict affirmative answers to instances of actual deployment of the gun to prevent or abort the commission of a crime that would otherwise have occurred. Second, the very small sample exposes the estimate to a large variance.

Professor Kleck revised his first estimate based on a survey conducted by him of approximately 5,000 randomly selected households in the continental United States. Based on an affirmative answer from 1.33% of respondents—again about 50 people—the resulting estimate of overall defensive use increased to as many as 2.4 million cases of defensive use of firearms.

Our best estimate then is that, considering civilians and law enforcement personnel together, approximately 82,000 persons use firearms each year in defense of person or property. This considerable incidence of defensive use must, however, be put in the balance against an annual toll estimated at over 40,000 firearms deaths, 280,000 nonfatal firearm injuries (including both intentional and unintentional shootings), and over 900,000 violent crimes involving handguns alone.

BENEFITS AND COSTS OF DEFENSIVE GUN USE

The assessment of the net benefits and costs of defensive use of firearms, considered at the level of the individual, is a subject of very active ongoing research. It may be that the answer to the question differs with whether we are considering violence in the home or violence on the street.

Defensive use of a firearm appears to modify the outcome of a violent crime, but the overall effect is unclear. The Department of Justice reports that 20% of persons using a firearm to defend themselves suffered an injury, compared with nearly half of those using another or no weapon. However, the authors urge that "care should be used in interpreting these data" because other important factors are not included in the analysis. In particular, many of these events involve law enforcement personnel; the findings may not extend to civilians.

SELF-DEFENSE AGAINST CRIMES

National Crime Victimization Survey Estimates of Number of Self-Defensive Firearm Incidents, by Type of Crime

Type of Crime	No. of Incidents, 1987–1990	Mean No. of Incidents per Year
Rape*	7,552	1,880.00
Robbery	30,900	7,725.00
Assault	152,031	38,007.75
Personal larceny*	2,056	514.00
Burglary	34,259	8,564.75
Household larceny	28,139	7,034.75
Motor vehicle theft*	3,523	880.75
Total	258,460	64,615.00

*Estimate based on fewer than 10 sample cases.

David McDowall and Brian Wiersma, *American Journal of Public Health*, December 1994.

And a different picture emerges when both fatal and nonfatal injuries are considered. In one study of robbery, active resistance is associated with a risk for death approximately 14 times greater than seen with other responses. This rises to a 49-fold increase in risk in the case of commercial robbery. The particular importance of this is that robbery is the stranger-to-stranger crime responsible for about 75% of felony killings in the United States.

In addition, the ready availability of guns purchased for protection appears to provide a major source of weaponry for criminals. As Professor Wright has put it, "The approximately 72 million handguns currently possessed by legitimate private owners represent a potentially rich source for criminal handgun acquisition." This conclusion is based on his finding that, in his study of incarcerated juvenile offenders, direct theft constituted an important source of gun acquisition. More than half of his sample of juvenile inmates had stolen at least one gun during their criminal careers. Many other guns acquired by his survey respondents by means other than theft had undoubtedly been stolen at some earlier time. Perhaps the highest estimate of the importance of theft as a source of criminal handguns comes from Professor Wright's survey of incarcerated adult felons. He found that as many as 70% of the most recent handguns owned by this group were stolen.

The Department of Justice has estimated that 341,000 guns are stolen in the United States each year. This is widely believed to be an underestimate; the California Department of Justice estimates that there are 100,000 guns stolen in that state alone each year (CDOJ). While there have been well publicized cases involving the theft of thousands of guns from manufacturers, nearly two-thirds (64%) of gun thefts occur during household burglaries.

GUNS IN THE HOME

Let us consider violence in the home as a function of the defensive use of guns. If a gun is to be useful for protection, it must be readily available and loaded or capable of being loaded in a very short time. Any other circumstance would defeat much of its utility. In the home, this results in the common practice of storing one or more firearms loaded and not locked away. Gun owners who keep a gun for protection are more than twice as likely as others to store a gun both loaded and unlocked. This behavior does not appear to be amenable by modification by gun safety training; in fact, gun owners who have received firearm safety training are more likely than others to store a gun in this manner.

There is probably no longer grounds for serious debate over whether this storage pattern increases or decreases risk for a violent death in the home. In the case of accidental shootings, many studies have established that this storage pattern allows children to acquire loaded guns, too often with tragic results. Young children may not be able to distinguish between real guns and toys, and even if they are, may not appreciate the fatal consequences of gun play.

USE OF GUNS BY VICTIMS

National Crime Victimization Survey Estimates of Number of Self-Defensive Firearm Incidents, by Victim-Offender Relationship and by Use of Gun

	No. of Incidents, 1987–1990	Mean No. of Incidents per Year
Relationship between victim and offender		
Stranger	182,368	45,592.00
Casual acquaintance	23,003	5,750.75
Well known	24,955	6,238.75
Undetermined	28,134	7,033.50
Manner in which victim used firearm		
Discharged firearm	71,549	17,887.25
Used firearm only to threaten offender	186,911	46,727.75

David McDowall and Brian Wiersma, *American Journal of Public Health*, December 1994.

More telling evidence comes from a series of careful field studies conducted by Dr. Arthur Kellermann and his associates. These researchers obtained very detailed data on persons who had died from a gun homicide or suicide in the home, and compared this information with data obtained from representatives of persons living in the same neighborhood who had not suffered such a death. Dr. Kellermann's careful analysis took into consideration other factors known to be associated with risk for violent death in the home, such as alcohol and other drug use, a history of violence, and a history of mental illness. After adjusting for a multitude of such factors, these researchers found that possession of a gun in the home was associated with a 2.7-fold increase in risk for a gun homicide and a 4.8-fold increase in risk for death from gun suicide. Gun ownership was not associated with an increase in risk from homicide or suicide by other methods. In the case of suicide, where a more detailed analysis was possible, risk was further increased by ownership of a handgun, by keeping any gun loaded as opposed to keeping all guns unloaded, and by keeping any gun unlocked as opposed to keeping all guns locked up.

DOMESTIC VIOLENCE

In one study of domestic violence resulting in assault, violence involving firearms was 12 times as likely to result in death as was assaultive violence involving any other weapon or bodily force. The importance of easily available firearms in aggravating domestic violence is reflected by the fact that although the overall risk of homicide for women is substantially lower than that for men, their risk of being killed by a spouse or intimate acquaintance is higher. In particular, more than twice as many women are shot and killed by their husband or intimate acquaintance than are murdered by strangers using any method at all.

Violence in the home, whether assaultive or self-directed, is most often impulsive. Frequently, one or more participants is intoxicated. Recourse is made to whatever weapon is at hand. If that weapon is a firearm, the consequences of the incident are much more likely to be a serious or fatal injury than if any other weapon had been chosen.

"Although solid proof of the effect of concealed-carry laws in reducing violent crime is relatively recent, it has long been clear that they do not threaten public safety."

LEGALIZING CONCEALED WEAPONS MAKES SOCIETY SAFER

David B. Kopel

Since 1987, Florida residents have been able to legally carry concealed firearms for personal protection. In the following viewpoint, David B. Kopel contends that violent crime rates have decreased in Florida and other states that permit concealed weapons. He argues that criminals become more wary of attacking citizens if those individuals are likely to be armed. Furthermore, he maintains, a study in Florida found very few instances of criminal behavior by concealed-weapons permit holders. Kopel is the research director of the Golden, Colorado–based Independence Institute, a think tank that supports gun ownership as a civil liberty. He is also the author of *The Samurai, the Mountie, and the Cowboy: Should America Adopt the Gun Controls of Other Democracies?* and the editor of *Guns: Who Should Have Them?*

As you read, consider the following questions:

1. According to Kopel, how has the movement to permit carrying concealed weapons become a women's issue?
2. What is faulty about the study of concealed weapons by David McDowall and his colleagues, in Kopel's opinion?
3. How many permits for carrying a concealed gun in Florida have been revoked because the holder committed a violent crime, according to the author?

David B. Kopel, "The Untold Triumph of Concealed-Carry Permits," *Policy Review*, July/August 1996. Copyright ©1996 by The Heritage Foundation. Reprinted by permission of The Heritage Foundation.

In recent years, the debate over gun policy has been dominated by two federal initiatives: the Brady bill's waiting period for the purchase of handguns and the ban on so-called assault weapons. While these federal issues have riveted the nation's attention, however, a quiet revolution in gun policy has spread throughout the states.

In 1986, only a half-dozen states routinely issued permits for trained citizens to carry concealed handguns for personal protection. Most states gave police departments wide latitude to issue such permits, which were rarely given to persons other than retired police officers and people with political connections. Today, however, 30 states comprising half the nation's population grant concealed-carry permits to law-abiding citizens. In the long run, this movement will be far more significant than either the Brady waiting period (which expires in 1998) or the ban on certain semiautomatics (which expires in 2004).

FLORIDA LEADS THE WAY

This movement began in the early 1980s, when gun-rights activists in Florida joined with law-enforcement lobbies such as the Florida Chiefs of Police Association to reform the state's handgun law. They proposed legislation that entitled any citizen who clears a fingerprint-based background check and passes gun-safety classes to receive a permit to carry a concealed handgun for protection.

Although the legislature passed the concealed-carry bill several times, it was vetoed repeatedly by Democratic governor Bob Graham. But his successor, Republican governor Bob Martinez, signed the bill in 1987. Since then, a steady progression of states has adopted concealed-carry laws modeled on Florida's, and more are likely to follow.

Whenever a state legislature first considers a concealed-carry bill, opponents typically warn of horrible consequences: Permit holders will slaughter each other in traffic disputes, while would-be Rambos shoot bystanders in incompetent attempts to thwart crime. But within a year of passage, the issue usually drops off the news media's radar screen, while gun-control advocates in the legislature conclude that the law wasn't so bad after all.

In some respects, the concealed-carry movement has become a women's issue. In fact, about a quarter of those who apply for and receive carry permits are women. When Alaska governor Walter Hickel signed concealed-carry legislation in 1993, he explained that the constituents he found most compelling were "the women who called and said they worked late and had to cross dark parking lots, and why couldn't they carry a concealed gun?"

Leading advocates for concealed-carry laws include female victims of crime such as Suzanna Gratia Hupp, whose parents were murdered five years ago in a mass killing in Killeen, Texas; Rebecca John Wyatt, the founder of Safety for Women and Responsible Motherhood; and Marion Hammer, the new president of the National Rifle Association and an activist in the Florida concealed-carry debate. Hammer once brandished her handgun to ward off a gang of would-be robbers.

A SAFER SOCIETY

Has this movement toward concealed-carry laws made America safer or more dangerous? In an article for the *Tennessee Law Review*, historian Clayton Cramer and I examined homicide rates in states that had adopted concealed-carry laws, adjusted for the effects of national homicide trends. In all but one state we examined, homicide rates did not appear to change as a result of the laws. We saw fluctuations, of course, but nothing out of the ordinary.

Reprinted by permission of David Clark and *Policy Review* magazine.

The lone exception was Florida, where the murder rate started an immediate, steady decline. Before the law, Floridians were about 36 percent more likely to be murdered than other Americans; after a few years, the Florida rate was equal to or slightly less than the national rate. As for other violent crimes, Florida was the worst state in the nation both before and after the new law. Florida's overall violent-crime rate, however, rose much more slowly since 1987 than did the national violent-crime rate.

We also examined violent-crime data in California, where permit policies vary widely by county. Counties that issue permits liberally had lower violent-crime rates than counties with restrictive policies; restrictive counties had lower rates than counties with prohibitive policies. A graduate student at Southwest Texas State University compared states that adopted concealed-carry laws with demographically similar states that did not. This study found strong support for the hypothesis that concealed-carry laws reduce the homicide rate, and weak (but still positive) support for a reduction in robbery and serious assault.

Advocates of gun control sometimes cite a 1995 study of concealed-carry policies by three researchers from the University of Maryland. The study looked at five urban areas and found that in four of them, the handgun homicide rate rose after a concealed-carry law had been enacted. But David McDowall, one of the authors, says that the small set of data limits the conclusions to be drawn from the study. He also states that there is no evidence permit holders commit crimes. The study is a classic illustration of how changing the parameters of a "before-and-after" analysis can change the results. For each city, McDowall and his colleagues averaged the yearly crime rates from 1973 until the year before the law went into effect, and compared that figure to the average rate of all subsequent years. If, instead, we compare the year before the law went into effect with the most recent year for which we have complete data (1994), then the homicide rate declined in three of the five cities.

THE EFFECTS OF CONCEALED-CARRY LAWS

All of the research about concealed-carry laws has been eclipsed by a comprehensive study by University of Chicago law professor John Lott, with graduate student David Mustard. Examining crime data for 3,054 counties, Lott and Mustard found that while concealed-carry reform had little effect in rural counties, in urban counties reform was followed by a substantial reduction in homicide and other violent crimes such as robbery. At the same time, there was a statistically significant rise in non-confrontational property crimes, such as larceny and car theft. Apparently many criminals concluded that the risks of encountering a victim who could fight back had become too high.

Lott and Mustard estimated that if all states that did not have concealed-carry laws in 1992 adopted such laws, there would be approximately 1,800 fewer murders and 3,000 fewer rapes annually. Thus the adoption or improvement of concealed-carry laws in more than a dozen states since 1992 may be one of several causes for the current decline in murder rates.

Of course, data alone cannot measure the benefits of concealed-carry reform. If a gun permit helps a woman feel safe enough to go jogging, her increased sense of security is an important social benefit—even if she never has to draw a gun. If she does encounter a criminal, the chances are small that she will actually have to fire, and less than 1 percent that he will take the gun away. In the most thorough study ever done on this subject, Florida State University criminologist Gary Kleck found that most instances of a citizen drawing a gun in self-defense end with the assailant simply retreating.

Although solid proof of the effect of concealed-carry laws in reducing violent crime is relatively recent, it has long been clear that they do not threaten public safety. The most detailed information we have about the behavior of such permit holders comes from Dade County, Florida.

MIAMI'S STATISTICS

When Florida's law went into effect, Miami's police chief ordered his officers to compile detailed reports of all police encounters with permit holders. In Miami, the number of permits increased from 1,200 in September 1987 to 21,092 in August 1992, when the police department decided that the behavior of permit holders did not merit further study. In five years, permit holders were convicted in these instances of criminal misuse of a firearm: two cases of aggravated assault involving a firearm, one case of armed trespass, and one case of a motorist shooting at another driver. In addition, one permit holder unthinkingly attempted to enter the secure area at Miami's airport with a firearm in her purse, and another accidentally shot himself in the leg.

The Dade County police also recorded the following incidents involving defensive use of licensed concealed firearms: two robbery cases in which the permit holder produced a firearm and the robbers fled; two cases involving permit holders who intervened to attempt to stop a robbery, but the robbers were not apprehended (and no one else was hurt); one robbery victim whose gun was seized by the robber; a man who shot a pit bull that was attacking him; two cases of a citizen capturing a burglar; three cases of a burglar who was frightened off but

not captured; one case of thwarted rape; and a bail bondsman who fired two shots at a fleeing bail-jumper wanted for armed robbery. There were no reports of permit holders shooting innocent people by accident.

In Florida as a whole, 315,000 permits had been issued by December 31, 1995. Only five had been revoked because the permit holder committed a violent crime with a gun.

CRIME, DETERRENCE, AND CONCEALED HANDGUNS

Using cross-sectional time-series data for U.S. counties from 1977 to 1992, we find that allowing citizens to carry concealed weapons deters violent crimes and it appears to produce no increase in accidental deaths. If those states which did not have right-to-carry concealed gun provisions had adopted them in 1992, approximately 1,570 murders; 4,177 rapes; and over 60,000 aggravated assaults would have been avoided yearly. On the other hand, consistent with the notion of criminals responding to incentives, we find criminals substituting into property crimes involving stealth and where the probabilities of contact between the criminal and the victim are minimal. The largest population counties where the deterrence effect on violent crimes is greatest are where the substitution effect into property crimes is highest. Concealed handguns also have their greatest deterrent effect in the highest crime counties.

John R. Lott Jr. and David B. Mustard, prepublication manuscript, *Journal of Legal Studies*, 1997.

Permit holders are not angels, but they are an unusually law-abiding collection of citizens. In Florida, for example, permit holders are about 300 times less likely to perpetrate a gun crime than Floridians without permits. Florida's experience has been copied nationwide. This should not be at all surprising: A person could carry a concealed handgun without a permit and, unless he gives himself away by committing some other offense, he would never be caught. Hence permit applicants tend to be those citizens willing to pay a large fee (usually more than $100) to comply with a law they could probably break with impunity.

SUPPORT FOR CONCEALED WEAPONS

Although 1 to 4 percent of the adult population exercises the freedom to carry a handgun for protection, a much larger group believes they should have such a choice. Polls usually show that one-half to two-thirds of the population supports concealed-carry laws. Higher rates are reported when respondents are in-

formed about the various restrictions—such as training require-ments—typically included in concealed-carry laws. These laws appeal to citizens who object neither to gun ownership nor to the use of force in self-defense, yet welcome moderate regula-tion to screen out undesirables.

Similarly, law-enforcement organizations in many states have supported concealed-carry laws. In Colorado, 53 of the state's 63 sheriffs voluntarily issue carry permits to citizens who pass a background check—even in liberal Boulder County. As these peace officers recognize, the government cannot in practice guarantee the safety of citizens in their daily lives. Therefore government must not prevent a responsible, trained individual from seeking to protect herself.

The concealed-carry movement is based on the principle that responsible citizens should not expect government to provide them with the essentials of life. Providing for the safety of one's self and one's family is first of all a personal duty.

Of course, everyone is a potential beneficiary of concealed-carry reform. Since criminals do not know which of their po-tential victims may be armed, even persons without carry per-mits would enjoy increased safety from any deterrent effect. Moreover, a *Psychology Today* study of "good Samaritans" who came to the aid of violent-crime victims found that 81 percent were gun owners, and many of them carried guns in their cars or on their persons.

Concealed-carry reform is no panacea for the high rates of crime in this nation, but it will be an important component of an anticrime strategy based on the right and duty of good citi-zens to take responsibility for public safety.

> "Carrying a concealed handgun does not guarantee safety or protection. . . . In fact, carrying a concealed weapon makes you more vulnerable."

LEGALIZING CONCEALED WEAPONS DOES NOT MAKE SOCIETY SAFER

Coalition to Stop Gun Violence

The following viewpoint is compiled from two fact sheets published by the Coalition to Stop Gun Violence, an association of more than forty organizations whose goal is to ban the sale and ownership of handguns in the United States. The coalition maintains that laws allowing individuals to carry concealed weapons do not reduce gun-related crime and may even increase it. Moreover, the coalition contends, the gun lobby's support of concealed-carry laws is merely a marketing ploy designed to boost sales of handguns and accessories.

As you read, consider the following questions:

1. According to the coalition, what is the difference between "may need" and "shall use" laws?
2. Why might concealed-weapons laws cause criminals to behave more violently, in the coalition's opinion?
3. In what ways is carrying a concealed gun a stimulant to violent confrontation, according to the coalition?

Reprinted by permission of the Coalition to Stop Gun Violence from its two fact sheets "Carrying Concealed Weapons" and "Responses to Common Gun Lobby Claims About Concealed Carry," March 1996.

L aws that regulate carrying concealed weapons (CCW) have been hotly debated in states across the United States. Generally, CCW laws can be grouped into two different types. One type of legislation, known as "may need" laws, allow authorities to issue a license to carry a concealed weapon to persons who demonstrate a compelling need. The second type, known as "shall use" laws, are much more permissive. Many "shall use" laws require authorities to grant a license to carry a concealed handgun to almost any adult state resident who does not have a felony conviction or history of mental illness.

Claiming "an armed society is a polite society," the NRA [National Rifle Association] has set up a state-by-state campaign to pass these less restrictive "shall use" CCW laws. [As of August 1996], there are [31] states that have these laws in place. Though the NRA won this battle in six states in 1995, similar measures in seven other states have failed.

THE DANGER OF MORE PERMISSIVE CCW LAWS

Permissive CCW laws do not reduce gun violence. Although these laws are relatively new, preliminary research indicates that more relaxed concealed carry laws do not decrease gun related homicides and may very well increase them. Based on data collected from three states, University of Maryland researchers David McDowall, Colin Loftin and Brian Wiersema found that the homicide rates did not significantly drop in these states following the adoption of concealed carry laws. Instead, in three of the five cities studied these researchers found a statistically significant increase in the rate of gun related homicides—74% in Jacksonville, 43% in Jackson and 22% in Tampa.

Carrying a concealed weapon creates a false sense of security and diverts attention away from efforts to address the underlying problems of gun violence. Carrying a concealed handgun does not guarantee safety or protection. According to the FBI, there were 49 handgun murders for every one civilian justifiable homicide in 1994. In fact, carrying a concealed weapon makes you more vulnerable. Researcher Arthur Kellerman, Director of the Center for Injury Control at Emory University, warns, "If the bad guys know more people are carrying guns, they just might shoot first and reach for the wallet later."

The public does not support more permissive CCW laws. An April 1995 study, *Illinois Statewide Survey on Public Attitudes Toward Concealed Handguns*, found that more than 73% of Illinois residents do not think that citizens should be able to carry concealed weapons. A Michigan survey of 600 state residents found that 71% opposed making it easier for people to carry concealed weapons.

For the last several years handgun sales have been dramatically low. Recognizing that the market for handguns was saturated, the gun industry promoted CCW laws to increase their handgun sales. Advertisements by the gun industry indicate a marketing strategy which utilizes the pro-gun lobby's CCW rhetoric to sell handguns and accessories to carry handguns. The truth is that the gun industry is out to increase their profit margin and not the safety and well-being of your community. . . .

COMMON CLAIMS ABOUT CONCEALED CARRY

Society is safer if criminals don't know who is armed. If the intent of carrying weapons is to deter crime, then why conceal them? Clearly concealed handguns are not as effective a deterrent as visible weapons. Arguably, concealed weapons laws may cause criminals to behave more violently. A criminal may anticipate a victim is armed and shoot first. . . .

Guns are used in self-defense more than 2,000,000 times each year in the United States. This "statistic" is based on a "study" by Gary Kleck that was scientifically unsound. The 2,000,000 figure is a national estimate based on the responses of a small, unrepresentative sample to a phone survey. For the survey, people were asked if they had used a gun successfully in self-defense. The respondents were allowed to define the successful use of a gun in self-defense however they wished. This means that if a person heard a bump in the night, picked up their gun, and the bump went away, they could call the incident a successful use of their gun in self-defense.

This same study estimates 2,000 to 3,000 justifiable firearms homicides by civilians each year, which does not come close to matching reality. The FBI reports there were 260 justifiable handgun homicides by civilians in 1994. If the Kleck study were accurate, there would be thousands more justifiable handgun homicides than what actually occurs. . . .

The conditions under which force is justifiable are narrowly defined. In most states, the use of force is justifiable only when a person is threatened with serious bodily injury, which means one cannot shoot someone who is stealing one's car radio. Many states also require that if one has a chance to run out the back door, one must take it. Force is justifiable only as an option of last resort.

An armed society is a polite society. Research overwhelmingly demonstrates that an armed society is a violent society. The more guns we have on the street and in our homes, the more violence we see. Research shows that a gun in the home is 43 times more likely to be used against a friend, family member or yourself than it is to be used in self-defense against an intruder.

ACTING ON EXPERIENCE

There is no available evidence from any law enforcement group or agency indicating that permitting people to carry concealed weapons makes anyone safer. Confronted with this fact, supporters of [concealed-carry laws] fall back on two arguments. One is that a lot of people already carry concealed weapons, so we should just go ahead and make it legal. A lot of people already commit murder, but that doesn't justify legalizing it. The second argument is that the right to carry a gun will make people feel safer. But all the evidence shows the contrary. Convenience stores, which have a vast reservoir of experience with armed robbery, do not permit their employees to keep guns on the premises because their security experts have determined that if the employees are armed, they are more likely to be killed in a robbery.

Molly Ivins, *Liberal Opinion Week*, March 27, 1995.

The Second Amendment guarantees my right to carry a concealed weapon. The Second Amendment reads, "A well regulated militia being necessary to the security of a free state, the right of the people to keep and bear arms shall not be infringed." Clearly, the Second Amendment does not mention an individual right to carry a concealed weapon. Furthermore, the Supreme Court has declared that "The Second Amendment guarantees no right to keep and bear a firearm that does not have some reasonable relationship to the preservation or efficiency of a well regulated militia."

ESCALATING THE SITUATION

If people are armed, tragedies like the Long Island Railroad shooting [in which Colin Ferguson killed six commuters and wounded nineteen in December 1993] *would be avoided.* Over the past decade, a majority of states have allowed the carrying of concealed weapons. There is no evidence that the armed citizens are able to prevent such tragedies from occurring. Police report that there have been people armed while in a massacre who chose not to respond for many different reasons. Deciding when it is appropriate to respond with deadly force and responding effectively is difficult even for trained police officers. One survivor of the Long Island Railroad shooting, a Vietnam veteran, attests that, even with all of his combat experience and weapons training, if he had been armed, there was nothing he could have done.

Furthermore, one never knows when one's response with a weapon escalates a situation into a massacre. Too often, innocent people get caught in the cross-fire or an undercover cop gets mistaken for a criminal, even when well-trained police officers are involved. The idea that poorly trained, self-appointed vigilantes are running through our streets looking to become heroes should not make any of us feel safer.

A gun is an equalizer for women to use against a male attacker. An unarmed woman who is sexually assaulted by an unarmed attacker has a 60 to 80% chance of escaping unraped and unharmed. If the woman or the attacker is armed, the chance that the woman is raped or harmed increases dramatically. Virtually all self-defense experts (except those employed by the NRA) specifically advise against owning a gun for self-protection because guns are so dangerous.

I'd rather have a gun and not need it than need a gun and not have it. Studies overwhelmingly demonstrate that the presence of gun is a stimulant to increased violence. This is called a "weapons effect." Guns make people cocky and more aggressive. Not only do people take risks they would not normally take, but they fail to take precautions. Instead of avoiding dark alleys, a person carrying a gun is more likely to initiate or escalate a confrontation.

The state of Florida enacted CCW in October 1987. The homicide rate per 100,000 in 1994 is 29% lower than the rate in 1986. The average homicide rate in Florida from 1988 to 1994 was 16% lower than the 1986 rate. However, Florida's average violent crime rate increased 13% over the same period. From these statistics it is impossible to establish any causation between the concealed carry laws and the increase and decrease of crime rates.

Arming a society does not create civility nor does it produce solutions to gun violence. We cannot solve our society's epidemic of violence by arming ourselves to the teeth.

PERIODICAL BIBLIOGRAPHY

The following articles have been selected to supplement the diverse views presented in this chapter. Addresses are provided for periodicals not indexed in the *Readers' Guide to Periodical Literature*, the *Alternative Press Index*, the *Social Sciences Index*, or the *Index to Legal Periodicals and Books*.

Cynthia Fuchs Epstein — "Pistol-Packing Mamas," *Dissent*, Fall 1995. Available from 521 Fifth Ave., New York, NY 10017.

Steve Fishman — "What You Know About Guns Can Kill You," *Vogue*, October 1993.

Liam T.A. Ford — "Gunning for Change," *Reason*, August/September 1994.

Ann Jones — "Living with Guns, Playing with Fire," *Ms.*, May/June 1994.

Paul Kirchner — "Defending Gun Ownership," *Chronicles*, February 1994. Available from 934 N. Main St., Rockford, IL 61103-7061.

Paxton Quigley and Dave Kopel — "You Can't Beat an (Armed) Woman," *Gun News Digest*, Summer 1995. Available from PO Box 488, Station C, Buffalo, NY 14209.

Charley Reese — "The Responsibility of Owning a Gun," *Conservative Chronicle*, January 24, 1996. Available from Box 29, Hampton, IA 50441.

Ruth Rosen — "Domestic Disarmament: A Women's Issue?" *Dissent*, Fall 1993.

Sojourners — "Annie Get Your Gun," March 1994. Available from 2401 15th St. NW, Washington, DC 20009.

Daniel Voll — "The Right to Bear Sorrow," *Esquire*, March 1995.

CHAPTER 4

WHAT MEASURES WOULD REDUCE GUN VIOLENCE?

CHAPTER PREFACE

It is a tragedy that makes the news all too often. A suspected criminal grabs a police officer's gun and pulls the trigger. Experts estimate that one in six law enforcement officers killed by a firearm is shot with his or her own gun. But scientists at the Sandia National Laboratories in Albuquerque are working to lower those statistics by developing "smart guns" that will not fire for anyone but their authorized shooters. In development are guns that will recognize their owners' fingerprints or voices. Others require wristbands or rings that emit radio signals that are picked up by a receiver in the gun's magazine. Colt Manufacturing hopes to begin selling a .40-caliber semiautomatic pistol that uses radio technology to law enforcement officers by 1997, as well as more sophisticated weapons by the year 2000.

Many gun-control advocates applaud the emergence of this smart technology. At a September 1996 news conference that showcased Colt's new smart gun, Pat Schroeder, a former U.S. representative from Colorado, said, "It is not enough to be tougher on crime; we have to be smarter. Crime-fighting technology is not just for James Bond. It should be available to our cops on the street." Other supporters contend that when the smart gun technology becomes available to the general public, handguns will become less attractive to thieves, especially if tampering with the safety system will permanently disable the gun.

However, some gun-control advocates are uneasy about the new technology. They fear that gun owners will become lax about gun safety if they think the technology will protect them from harm. The National Rifle Association is also ambivalent about smart guns. While the organization maintains that it welcomes any technology that makes guns safer, it also fears that Congress will require all future guns to be equipped with smart technology. With a surcharge of 10 to 50 percent of the firearm's cost for this technology, the NRA contends, the technology will price the guns out of the reach of many Americans who want to own a firearm.

Much of the debate over gun control in America centers around which measures, if any, would reduce crime and gun violence. The authors in the following chapter examine the potential effects of gun-control laws and other measures designed to decrease violent crime.

"If we don't get tougher about gun control, then we shouldn't be surprised by the number of corpses we accumulate."

GUN CONTROL WILL REDUCE VIOLENT CRIME

Raymond W. Kelly

Raymond W. Kelly is the undersecretary for enforcement at the U.S. Treasury Department and a former police commissioner of New York City. The following viewpoint is an excerpt of a speech Kelly gave at an FBI symposium in Quantico, Virginia, on February 16, 1993, in which he argues that Americans have become too tolerant of lenient gun laws and too accustomed to violent crime. Gun-control measures such as mandatory waiting periods, bans on assault rifles, limits on gun and ammunition purchases, and registration of all handguns slow the flow of guns into the hands of criminals and reduce gun-related crime and violence, Kelly maintains.

As you read, consider the following questions:
1. According to Kelly, how does America's homicide rate compare to the homicide rates of Canada and Japan?
2. What are two indications that Americans are becoming too tolerant of crime and violence, in the author's opinion?
3. How many people were killed by handguns in 1992, according to Kelly?

Excerpted from "Toward a New Intolerance," a speech by Raymond W. Kelly to the Second Annual FBI National Symposium on Addressing Violent Crime Through Community Involvement, Quantico, Va., February 16, 1993.

I believe the fight against crime in America, like that against Soviet domination, is now essentially a fight for freedom.

Fearing crime, or becoming one of its victims, is to lose a fair measure of freedom in a democratic society. And my premise today is that we have gotten far too accustomed to, and accepting of, crime and violence. The public and law enforcement alike have acquired a new tolerance to both. Why? Perhaps the numbers are just too overwhelming. Perhaps it's because we know that law enforcement can't work miracles. We know that the problems that land on the doorstep of law enforcement stem from vast social failures that the police alone will never solve.

Yet the police can't withdraw either. We are engaged in addressing society's worst problems, and the public looks to us for solutions. They look to us for leadership. We can ill afford to become numb to violence and the community erosion it causes. People rely on the police to make a difference.

I believe the vehicles to help us regain some ground over violent crime are there. One is gun control and the other is community policing. We need to focus on both to make the kind of breakthrough that will make measurable differences in public safety.

VIOLENCE BECOMES ACCEPTABLE

There's no doubt about how violent we've become. The annual homicide rate in America is now about 22 for every 100,000 Americans. In Canada the rate is three for every 100,000 Canadians. In Japan, it is less than one. The fact is we have become too tolerant of murder. In New York City, there has somehow arisen a new benchmark for homicides: Over 2,000 homicides a year is considered bad. Up to 2,000 is, well, somehow "expected," or acceptable. The old chestnut of laying things end-to-end to get a sense of proportion becomes frighteningly macabre when you realize that 2,000 bodies end-to-end would stretch for over two miles.

So, of course, it is not acceptable. Just as it is not acceptable that our national homicide rate is seven times greater than that of our Canadian neighbors. It is never acceptable. It is simply familiar. We have grown accustomed to the staggering numbers.

We were not always as tolerant. In the Winter 1993 issue of the American Scholar, Senator Daniel Patrick Moynihan writes how shocked the America of 1929 was when seven mobsters were murdered one St. Valentine's Day. "It would appear," Senator Moynihan wrote, "that the society in the 1920s was simply not willing to put up with this degree of deviancy." But now, it seems, we are. Last Sunday, Valentine's Day 1993, we had 12 homicides in New York City; three in one apartment in Brooklyn, six in one apartment in the Bronx, and the rest at various locations. The fact is our larger cities regularly reach a body count of a half-dozen or more over two- and three-day periods, but rarely do we call them massacres anymore.

THE EROSION OF FREEDOM

Society's increasing tolerance to crime and antisocial behavior in general is abetting our own enslavement. The erosion of freedom caused by crime is so pervasive that we are in danger of failing to notice it at all. It is accepted practice that the elderly, certainly, stay home at night. They are easy prey so they make themselves scarce. They check before getting into elevators. Women of all ages take similar precautions. And, increasingly, we worry about our children's safety going to and from school. And even in school.

THE RIGHT LAWS

An effective body of firearms laws must recognize an obvious truth obscured thus far by our cultural indulgence in the romance of guns and the effective propaganda of the gun lobby: when guns are easy to get, the wrong people get them easily.

Buying a gun should be the most difficult consumer ritual in America, instead of one of the easiest. Toughening acquisition will not harm legitimate gun owners. The right laws, in fact, can only help them. The right laws can reduce the incidence of impulsive teenage suicides. The right laws can limit the firepower of street guns and undoubtedly save the lives of a few innocent bystanders. . . .

Most important, toughening the process will staunch the free flow of weapons to the bad guys and others who simply should not own guns.

Erik Larson, Lethal Passage: How the Travels of a Single Handgun Expose the Roots of America's Gun Crisis, 1994.

No one is immune. A New York City police officer who chased a troublesome teenager away from a school was shot the next day by the same boy who ambushed him from a nearby rooftop. When the boy observed that he wounded the police officer in the foot, he complained to a friend that "I wanted to get him in the cabbage. . ." meaning the head. Yet we seem to be growing immune to the existence of such sociopaths.

There is an expectation of crime in our lives. We are in danger of becoming captive to that expectation, and to the new tolerance to criminal behavior, not only in regard to violent crime. A number of years ago there began to appear in the windows of automobiles parked on the streets of American cities signs which read: "No Radio." Rather than express outrage, or even annoyance at the possibility of a car break-in, people tried to communicate with the potential thief in conciliatory terms. The translation of "No Radio" is: "Please break into someone else's car, there's nothing in mine." These "No Radio" signs are flags of urban surrender. They are hand-written capitulations. Instead of "No Radio," we need new signs that say "No Surrender."

Another disturbing indicator of our new tolerance has to do with the omnipresence of guns. We see it in people who show up at community meetings to ask if the Police Department can help get metal detectors installed in their schools. When people ask for metal detectors the way they used to ask for more library books, then you know your tolerance level is way too high. For certain, we have become far too tolerant of guns. The police and public should insist on a new level of tolerance. And we should insist that Congress adopt the strictest gun control measures possible. . . .

GUN CONTROL IS NECESSARY

Now is the time for Congress to end all the talk on gun control and enact any number of measures to stop the carnage that guns—especially handguns—are causing. Those of us in law enforcement need to play an important role in that regard. It is time to call the bluff of the vaunted gun lobby. We should hold it accountable—at least, in part, for the mounting body count. The gun lobby talks about individual freedom. But they help rob us of freedom. Certainly, the freedom from fear. They fill the halls of Congress with the rhetoric of liberation. But who is liberated when arsenals for drug dealers, street gangs and psychopaths are protected? The fact is the number of guns in private hands about doubles in America every 20 years to the point where there are now over 200 million guns in circulation. That compares to 54 million in 1950.

Right now, there exist well-known proposals that might begin to stem the flood of guns into illegal use. They include the Brady bill [passed by Congress in November 1993], the banning of assault rifles [passed by Congress in August 1994], and the limitation on some ammunition. Isn't it also time to seriously consider the central registration of all handguns? We register cars everywhere in America. And information about those cars is available through a nationwide computer link.

Why not handguns? There are Federal restrictions and permit requirements for machine guns. But not handguns. Even though handguns are doing most of the blood-letting. National registration will help us trace how guns that are supposed to be sold legally end up in illegal hands. Would it be expensive? Probably. But not nearly as costly as the 22,000 lives lost in 1992 from handguns. National registration would produce a trail of ownership. It would produce an interesting trail of civil liability, as well, for persons who sold or disposed of their guns illegally or just recklessly.

OTHER ALTERNATIVES

We need to explore all of these alternatives, and more. We confiscated nearly 20,000 illegal guns in New York City last year. Ninety percent of them come from easy-to-purchase states with registration requirements that are nonexistent or dubious at best. I applaud Governor Douglas Wilder and those state legislators who recognize the problem and are trying to bring it under control in Virginia. Shouldn't we consider making it a federal offense to commit a crime with a gun obtained in one state and used in another? There is certainly an interstate nexus that would form the basis for such a law.

GUN CONTROL MEANS FEWER CRIMES

Consider the experience of the many foreign nations that tightly restrict private gun ownership: Those that limit firearms control gun violence more effectively. Gun crime is by no means unheard of in these nations, but even with a black market trade and homemade weapons, the incidence of gun homicide, accidents, armed robberies and other violent crimes is much lower than here.

Los Angeles Times, December 28, 1993.

Eliminating the abuse of the Federal Firearm License is another area to explore. Over 600 such licenses have been issued to people in New York City who have no retail outlet whatsoever, and who have no New York City gun license. In other words, over 600 individuals have received licenses from the Federal government to help them break the law in New York. Let me quickly add, however, that both the New York City Police Department and the Bureau of Alcohol, Tobacco and Firearms recognize the problem and are working jointly to correct it. The

Police Department is adding officers to an existing NYPD-ATF Joint Firearms Task Force to track down Federal Firearms Licensees who are suspected of bringing guns into New York City in violation of local statutes.

If we don't get tougher about gun control, then we shouldn't be surprised by the number of corpses we accumulate. Gun control laws, the stricter the better, are critical. . . .

TOUGH LAWS ARE NEEDED

I urge that all of us in this room today commit ourselves to passage of the toughest laws possible. If it means banning some guns outright, then help ban them. If it means central registration for all others, then help require registration. If it means limiting the frequency of gun purchases, then help limit them. If it means waiting periods, then help make them wait.

The point is, as law enforcement executives and concerned citizens, you can help deliver a message to Congress. And that message is: Do something! We need to "do something" to develop a new intolerance to crime and violence. We need to "do something," or lose our freedom to crime and violence. We need to tear up our "No Radio" signs and reclaim some dignity. We can be slaves to our metal detectors and car alarms, or we can stage a revolt. I'm for staging a revolt.

"Gun control laws hinder and harass ordinary citizens while doing virtually nothing to (except sometimes assisting) criminal predators."

GUN CONTROL DOES NOT REDUCE VIOLENT CRIME

Robert W. Lee

In the following viewpoint, Robert W. Lee asserts that gun-control laws encourage crime and violence. These measures prevent law-abiding citizens from keeping firearms to defend themselves but do not prevent criminals from obtaining guns illegally, he argues. When criminals know their potential victims are unarmed, Lee maintains, they are free to commit crimes with impunity. Only when the populace is armed are criminals deterred and the crime rate lowered, he contends. Lee is a frequent contributor to the *New American*, a conservative magazine.

As you read, consider the following questions:

1. According to Lee, what was the result when Evanston, Illinois, imposed a near-total ban on handgun possession?
2. Why are waiting periods for handgun purchases a bad idea, in Lee's opinion?
3. What was the effect of New York's Sullivan law, according to the author?

Robert W. Lee, "Protecting Life and Property," *New American*, April 4, 1994. Reprinted with permission.

Year after year, despite the investment of astronomical sums of tax money to "fight crime," the battle is far from won. In response to the high crime rate, advocates of big government offer, among other counterproductive "solutions," more gun controls, thereby further increasing the ratio of guns in the hands of government and the criminal underworld to those available to ordinary citizens. It is no coincidence, as author Robert J. Kukla noted more than two decades ago in his comprehensive study, Gun Control, that "those who have sought the most in gun control have sought the least in the punishment of criminals," and have, at the same time, "been foremost in the aggravation of the conditions of crime which they say they deplore and which they pretend they seek to remedy."

Whereas gun controls nurture crime, the right to keep and bear arms properly exercised serves to protect individuals and communities from crime, and nations from tyranny. Gun control, after all, is not about the elimination of guns, but about who will control them. Guns would still exist even if they were outlawed, but in that event guns would become a virtual monopoly of government agents and common criminals, with the rest of society caught defenseless in the crossfire. Nobody in his right mind would put a sign on his front door proclaiming that "this house has no guns." Yet the elimination of guns in the hands of law-abiding citizens would in effect place such a sign on their homes.

A TALE OF TWO CITIES

As of 1990, the largest U.S. town to impose a near-total ban on handgun possession was the Chicago suburb of Evanston, Illinois. Evanston adopted its handgun ban on September 13, 1982, and Florida State University criminologist Dr. Gary Kleck reports that for "the three crime categories that involve gun use with any frequency [murder and non-negligent manslaughter, armed robbery, and aggravated assault], the data indicate that Evanston experienced increases in all three categories from 1982 to 1983," suggesting "that even the toughest gun law on the book failed to reduce violent crime."

In sharp contrast, the Atlanta suburb of Kennesaw, Georgia, also passed a city gun ordinance in 1982—one that requires heads of households (with certain exceptions) to keep at least one firearm in their homes. Though the penalty for violation is minimal, and there has been no attempt to enforce the statute, the improvement in the city's crime statistics is startling. During the law's first year, crimes against persons (including homicide, rape, armed robbery, aggravated assault, and residential burglary) plummeted 74 percent compared to 1981, then dropped another 45 percent in 1983 compared to 1982. Crime has remained remarkably low ever since, despite a population increase from around 5,000 in 1980 to more than 10,000 today. There were only 46 burglaries (both business and residential) during 1993. For the 11-year period 1983–93, armed robberies averaged a mere 1.6 annually, rapes 1.5, and murders 0.2. There have been no murders with firearms since the pro-gun ordinance went into effect. The city's only two homicides were committed with knives.

THE GREAT EQUALIZER

Dr. Kleck completed a study indicating that guns are used in self-defense between 800,000 and 2.4 million times annually. In more than 90 percent of these cases, no one is injured or killed. And in most instances when shots are fired, the purpose is merely to frighten the assailants into retreating.

TIMELESS WISDOM

Thomas Jefferson (quoting Cesare Beccaria) once wrote that "laws that forbid the carrying of arms . . . disarm only those who are neither inclined nor determined to commit crimes. Such laws make things worse for the assaulted and better for the assailants; they serve rather to encourage than to prevent homicides, for an unarmed man may be attacked with greater confidence than an armed man."

The rampant violent crime occurring in our gun-controlled urban centers certainly proves this timeless wisdom to be correct.

Michael J. Kumeta, *San Diego Union-Tribune*, June 25, 1995.

For instance, on February 22, 1991, a man walked into the Millcreek Pharmacy and Hardware store in Murray, Utah, and handed pharmacist Rod Dunn a note asserting, "I am an addict. I have a gun. Be smart and no one will get hurt." The note demanded two pain-killers, which the robber successfully obtained. Thirteen days later, the same thug returned for a refill, telling Mr. Dunn, "Okay, let's do this one more time." But this time Dunn was ready. Pulling a .22-calibre revolver from under the counter and pointing it at the robber, Dunn declared, "I don't know if you have a gun, but I have one," at which point the suspect ran from the store. Dunn gave chase and fired a warning shot into a fence the fleeing malefactor was climbing.

Although the suspect escaped, Dunn told the *New American* that there have been no further robbery attempts since.

What carrying a concealed firearm can mean when the chips are down and the police are not around was demonstrated on December 30, 1992, when 75-year-old Michael Baranelli visited the barbershop in Birmingham, Alabama, that he had patronized for some 40 years. Baranelli, another customer, and the shop owner were the only ones present when two thugs armed with .38-calibre pistols entered the shop and demanded valuables. The three complied, and Baranelli later told reporters that if "they had taken the money and walked out the door, that would have been the end of it. We'd have lost some money and been glad not to get killed."

Instead, one of the robbers asked, "Do you want to die?", his accomplice echoed the question, and the would-be victims were ordered to lie on the floor. At that point, Baranelli, who has held a permit to carry a concealed firearm for over 40 years, became convinced that they were going to die unless prompt action was taken. Baranelli had a two-shot, .22-calibre Derringer in his pocket that the *Birmingham News* later described, without much exaggeration, as a "peashooter." When the gunman standing directly in front of Baranelli momentarily turned to glance at his partner some eight or nine feet away, Baranelli quickly pulled the pistol from his pocket and, in a fraction of a second, shot both robbers. One died instantly and the other was knocked unconscious. Baranelli was able to save three innocent lives, including his own, because he was armed.

BRADY MADNESS

During his confirmation hearings on July 29, 1993, FBI Director Louis J. Freeh endorsed the Brady waiting-period bill. Exactly one month earlier, on June 29, 1993, 21-year-old Woodbridge, Virginia, resident Rayna Ross awoke at 3:00 a.m. to discover that ex-boyfriend Anthony Goree had forced his way into her apartment armed with a bayonet. With death possibly imminent, Ross pulled out the .38-calibre pistol she had purchased for protection only three days earlier and shot her assailant twice, mortally wounding him. Had a Brady-type waiting period been in effect at the time, Ross may well have been murdered, since, as the *Washington Times* for July 13, 1993, noted editorially, she had bought her gun "just one full business day before the attack came." And if "Ms. Ross lived in the District of Columbia, where handguns are banned, she would also be dead."

Not so fortunate was Bonnie Elmasri of Wauwatosa, Wisconsin. As reported in the May 14, 1993, issue of the *Gun Owners*, official newsletter of Gun Owners of America, Elmasri in 1991 "tried to buy a gun to protect herself from her estranged husband," but she "had to wait 48 hours before she could pick it up." Unfortunately, she never did so, as she and her two sons "were murdered the next day by an abusing husband of whom the police were well aware."

No Persuasive Evidence

Sociology professor James D. Wright and his colleagues were asked to survey the state of research regarding the efficacy of gun control, presumably to show that gun control worked and that America needed more of it. But when the researchers produced their report for the National Institute of Justice in 1982, they delivered a document quite different from the one they had expected to write. Carefully reviewing all existing research, the three scholars found no persuasive scholarly evidence that America's 20,000 gun-control laws had reduced criminal violence. For example, the federal Gun Control Act of 1968, which banned most interstate gun sales, had no discernible impact on the criminal acquisition of guns from other states. Washington, D.C.'s ban on the ownership of handguns that had not already been registered in the District was not linked to any reduction in gun crime. Even Detroit's law providing mandatory sentences for felonies committed with a gun was found to have no effect on gun-crime patterns, in part because judges would often reduce the sentence for the underlying offense in order to balance out the mandatory two-year extra sentence for use of a gun.

David B. Kopel, *Policy Review*, Winter 1993.

Former Assistant Secretary of the Treasury Paul Craig Roberts speculates that the Brady law "will kill as many people as it will save. Waiting periods might prevent a few crimes of passion, but they also cause deaths by precluding self-defense." In addition, they divert scarce police resources from catching criminals to filling out paperwork.

Defenseless Victims

Most of the widely publicized incidents of mass-murder with firearms have entailed a group of defenseless victims facing an armed lawbreaker. After racist gunman Colin Ferguson killed six persons and wounded 17 others on a crowded New York commuter train on December 7, 1993, President Bill Clinton and other gun control lobbyists jumped on the incident to call for additional gun controls. Yet it was New York's Sullivan law, which precludes the carrying of concealed weapons by ordinary citizens, that assured there would be no one on the train adequately prepared to defend against Ferguson's attack. (For his part, Ferguson had obtained his gun legally in California after passing the Golden State's 15-day waiting period.)

Similarly, on October 16, 1991, George Jo Hennard killed 23 persons and wounded some 20 others at a cafeteria in Killeen, Texas, before killing himself. Had just one victim been armed, he could have been stopped after relatively few casualties. Dr. Suzanna Gratia's mother and father were among his victims. Dr. Gratia, who was authorized to carry a gun in her automobile, but barred by state law from carrying it in her purse, later recalled that when she realized what was going on she "reached for my purse—I used to carry a gun in it. The gun was out in my car. . . . My anger, honestly, has turned toward legislators who have legislated me out of carrying my gun for my protection." Except for the gun control statute, "that gun would have been in my purse. I'm not saying I could have saved everybody in there, but I would have felt like I had a chance. . . ."

Contrast the carnage wrought by Ferguson and Hennard with another incident that occurred near midnight on December 18, 1991, in Anniston, Alabama. Three armed robbers entered a Shoney's restaurant and began herding some 20 employees and patrons into a walk-in cooler. After closing the door, and while holding the manager at gunpoint, one of the thugs noticed a patron hiding under a nearby table and began shooting at what the thug apparently presumed was a defenseless victim. But Thomas Glen Terry was carrying a .45-calibre semiautomatic handgun for which he had a permit. Terry returned the fire, killing one of the robbers and critically wounding another, while the third fled. While Terry received a slight wound, the employees and other customers were unhurt. An Anniston police lieutenant was quoted as saying that Terry "is not a security guard or a police officer or anything that would call for him to carry a weapon that way, but I understand he carried it pretty much at all times." For which at least 20 of his fellow citizens, to say nothing of his own loved ones, are very grateful.

WEAPONS ROUNDUP

May 1, 1993, was Regional Gun Turn-In Day throughout crime-plagued Metropolitan Washington, DC. The stated purpose of this event was to get weapons out of homes and off the streets by having residents of the area surrender firearms to the police.

Around 300 guns were collected. Needless to say, there was no evidence that any members of Washington's flourishing criminal community surrendered their weapons.

Luckily, one unidentified 52-year-old District resident did not participate in the ludicrous disarmament drive. Two days later, three youths knocked on his door and asked for some water to cool what they claimed was an overheated car engine. The homeowner gave them a bucketful but, taking no chances, placed the illegal handgun he had secured for self-protection on a shelf beside the door as the youths went to their car. When they returned with the empty bucket, one pulled a handgun and told the homeowner to raise his hands, which he did, and in the process retrieved the handgun he had sequestered on the shelf. The homeowner shot the gun-wielding thug, the other two fled, and the would-be victim, now safely in control of the situation, called the police. Had he turned in his gun two days earlier as the anti-gun zealots had urged, he might instead have been killed and would unquestionably have been the victim of a violent crime. The police confiscated the handgun which the assailant had brandished, but also the one with which the homeowner had defended his life, since he was not supposed to have it under the District's stringent gun control statutes. Big-hearted authorities did say, however, that the man would not be prosecuted.

Commenting on the incident, the May 7, 1993, *Washington Times* editorialized that "guns in private hands can be and are effective in protecting their owners from crime and in preventing crime. Criminals know this; they avoid houses and places where they think there are guns. The only people who don't know it are the misguided and ill-informed do-gooders who want you to disarm yourself by throwing away your guns and making others throw away theirs—except the real criminals, who will not comply with these laws anyway."

ASSISTING CRIMINALS

As noted earlier, gun control laws hinder and harass ordinary citizens while doing virtually nothing to (except sometimes assisting) criminal predators. In fact, New York's Sullivan law, which helped make the commuter train safe for Colin Ferguson, was actually adopted in 1911 to help, not hinder, lawbreakers. Although it was sold to residents of the state as a crime-stopper, within two years the *New York Times* lamented (May 24, 1913) that "criminals are as well armed as ever" and acknowledged that it was "a fact too obvious for denial" that "the concealed weapon law has not worked as well as expected, or at any rate hoped, by those of us who commended it in principle. . . ." Which should have come as no surprise, since, as Paul Craig Roberts has noted, Timothy D. Sullivan, for whom the law was named, "was a member of the State Assembly who represented the Red Hook district of Brooklyn. This district surrounds the Gowanus Canal. It was a hotbed of crime in the late 19th century and remains a dangerous place today. Many of Red Hook's inhabitants made their living from robbing the docks and warehouses and assaulting persons from other parts of the city who had to pass through the district. To protect against robberies, owners armed their dock workers, and persons who had to pass through the district began carrying weapons. These acts of self-protection caused a sharp drop in robberies."

From the thugs' perspective, however, some help was needed. Roberts continues: "Red Hook's criminals persuaded Sullivan to introduce and secure the passage of a law that disarmed the public so that robberies could not be prevented by armed resistance. The purpose of the Sullivan law was to protect the criminal," a purpose it has served for nearly a century.

After the CBS program *Street Stories* broadcast a segment on "Women and Guns" in 1993, producer Jill Fieldstein received a note from a Nevada viewer, to whom she responded on April 29, 1993: "As a card carrying member of the liberal media, producing this piece was an eye opening experience. I have to admit that I saw guns as inherently evil, violence begets violence, and so on. I have learned, however, that in trained hands, just the presence of a gun can be a real 'man stopper.' I am sorry that women have had to resort to this, but . . . wishing it wasn't so won't make it any safer out there."

Perhaps there is hope!

VIEWPOINT

3

"The [Brady] law has been responsible
for stopping tens of thousands of
felons ... from buying handguns. ...
Undoubtedly, many American lives
are being saved as a result."

WAITING PERIODS WILL REDUCE THE NUMBER OF CRIMINALS WHO OBTAIN HANDGUNS

Handgun Control, Inc.

Handgun Control, Inc., is an organization that advocates strict gun-control laws. In the following viewpoint, the organization maintains that the Brady law's mandatory five-day waiting period and background check for handgun sales is an effective means of keeping guns out of the hands of criminals. A survey by Handgun Control, Inc., shows that since the law was passed, thousands of felons have been prevented from buying handguns from gun dealers, and many fugitives have been arrested due to background checks. Preventing criminals from buying handguns will decrease the number of Americans who die as a result of gun violence, the organization contends.

As you read, consider the following questions:
1. What was the denial rate for handgun purchases under the Brady law in 1994 and 1995, according to Handgun Control, Inc.?
2. According to Handgun Control, Inc., the 1994 crime bill added what group of people to those who are prohibited from buying a handgun under the Brady law?
3. What is the primary purpose of the Brady law, according to the organization?

From pages 1-2 of "The Brady Law: Still Effective After Twenty-Two Months," a publication of Handgun Control, Inc. Reprinted with permission.

A fter more than seven years of debate, Congress passed the Brady Bill in 1993 and President Bill Clinton signed it into law on November 30, 1993. On February 28, 1994, the waiting period and mandatory background check on handgun purchasers went into effect nationwide. A background check identifies those persons prohibited by law from purchasing a handgun, such as convicted felons, fugitives from justice, drug addicts, illegal aliens, juveniles and those adjudicated mentally ill. Critics argued that felons and other prohibited persons did not purchase handguns over the counter from legitimate gun dealers. Police chiefs and other law enforcement officials knew better. The Brady Law has proven law enforcement correct and the critics wrong.

THE BRADY LAW'S EFFECTIVENESS

The Brady Law does not require law enforcement agencies to compile or maintain records on the aggregate number of applications or denials, but voluntary reporting gives some indication of the law's effectiveness. On February 28, 1995, Handgun Control, Inc. (HCI) and the International Association of Chiefs of Police released the results of a survey of 115 law enforcement agencies that showed that during the first year of the Brady Law those 115 agencies conducted 572,224 background checks and denied 19,098 for a denial rate of 3.34%.

A follow-up telephone survey conducted by HCI collected 1995 data for 22 law enforcement agencies in 15 states. The aggregate totals showed:

- 470,470 background checks conducted;
- 14,925 denials;
- 3.17% denial rate.

Clearly, thousands of ineligible purchasers are being prevented from buying handguns from gun dealers. The Colorado Department of Public Safety, for example, stopped 1,324 persons charged with or convicted of a violent felony offense from purchasing handguns during 1995 and 1,657 persons charged with or convicted of non-violent felonies.

As part of the Crime Bill signed into law by President Clinton in September 1994, federal law was amended to prohibit persons under a domestic violence restraining order from purchasing a handgun. This class was added to prevent domestic abusers and stalkers from buying handguns. The HCI survey reveals that at least two jurisdictions are denying significant numbers of people under domestic violence restraining orders from buying handguns. The Kentucky State Police denied 323 individuals and the Colorado Department of Public Safety denied 72 such individuals from purchasing handguns. Other jurisdictions report that they need improved record keeping systems in order to adequately screen out stalkers and others under a domestic violence restraining order from buying handguns.

1995 BRADY LAW BACKGROUND CHECKS

Department	Number of Brady Checks	Number of Denials	Percentage
Arizona Department of Public Safety	88,668	2,229	2.51%
Arkansas State Police Department	28,298	537	1.90%
Colorado Department of Public Safety	52,894	3,373	6.38%
Idaho Department of Law Enforcement	28,633	883	3.08$
Kentucky State Police	59,500	1,129	1.90%
Nevada Highway Patrol	31,067	552	1.78%
South Carolina Department of Law Enforcement	53,157	2,106	3.96%
Utah Department of Public Safety	33,314	560	1.68%
West Virginia State Police	25,288	187	0.74%
Albuquerque (NM) Police Department	4,521	163	3.61%
Amarillo (TX) Police Department	2,532	52	2.05%
Choctaw (OK) Police Department	85	1	1.18%
Corpus Christi (TX) Police Department	3,218	166	5.16%
Dallas (TX) Police Department	12,994	921	7.09%
El Paso (TX) Police Department	4,774	220	4.61%
New Orleans (LA) Police Department	11,237	1,124	10.00%
Oklahoma City (OK) Police Department	14,130	252	1.78%
Plano (TX) Police Department	2,093	52	2.48%
San Antonio (TX) Police Department	10,122	210	2.07%
Shawnee County (KS) Sheriff's Department	1,877	77	4.10%
Wyandotte County (KS) Sheriff's Department	1,370	92	6.72%
Yellowstone County (MT) Sheriff's Department	698	10	1.43%
Totals	470,470	14,896	3.17%

Handgun Control, Inc., *The Brady Law: Still Effective After Twenty-Two Months*, January 1996.

While "denials" are one indication of the Brady Law's effectiveness, many criminals are deterred from even attempting to buy a handgun. In other instances, criminals and convicted felons flee the gun store when informed about the Brady background check. The Utah Department of Public Safety, for example, reported that:

> One gentleman, all of a sudden, realized he had forgotten something at home when advised that an out-of-state record check is

part of the background check. His record showed he was currently under indictment for kidnapping.

Another person left the store before the transaction was completed and his record showed a felony conviction for the rape of a child.

The primary purpose of the Brady Law is to stop felons and other prohibited persons from making an over-the-counter purchase of a handgun. The law's background checks have led to the arrest of many fugitives. The Utah Department of Public Safety reports numerous examples of arrests resulting from Brady background checks, including the following:

Another subject trying to purchase a handgun from a pawn dealer was arrested by the Salt Lake City Police Department on a felony warrant out of Colorado for aggravated sexual abuse of a child. The pawn dealer stalled the subject until police could arrive.

In Alexandria, Louisiana, a man tried to purchase a handgun at a local store and submitted a Brady background check form. The local sheriff's office ran his name through the National Crime Information Computer and discovered a felony theft warrant for him from the state of Colorado. The Alexandria police arrested the man and extradited him to the Adams County Sheriff's office in Colorado.

The Brady Law has been in effect since February 28, 1994. Since its implementation, the law has been responsible for stopping tens of thousands of felons and other prohibited persons from buying handguns. Hundreds of fugitives are being caught and arrested as a result of Brady Law background checks. In at least two states, stalkers, domestic abusers and other violence-prone individuals who are under restraining orders are being stopped from buying handguns. Undoubtedly, many American lives are being saved as a result of the Brady Law.

"The five-day national waiting period has netted only four federal prosecutions of prohibited persons attempting to purchase a firearm."

WAITING PERIODS ARE INEFFECTIVE

Robert Hausman

In the following viewpoint, Robert Hausman argues that the Brady law—which instituted a mandatory five-day waiting period and a background check for over-the-counter handgun sales from licensed dealers—is ineffective. An overwhelming majority of handgun purchasers are qualified to buy handguns under the law, he maintains. Most of those whose applications were initially rejected, Hausman contends, were later found to be qualified to make handgun purchases. Hausman has written many articles on gun control and is a regular contributor to *Gun Week* and *Guns and Ammo* magazines.

As you read, consider the following questions:

1. By how much have criminal prosecutions of armed criminals dropped under the Clinton administration, according to the author?
2. According to Hausman, who is prohibited by federal law from purchasing firearms?
3. What do the results of the survey by Handgun Control, Inc., prove to the author?

From Robert Hausman, "Questions Raised on Brady Law's Effectiveness in Fighting Crime," *Gun News Digest*, April 7, 1995. Reprinted by permission of the author.

An examination on the effectiveness of the Brady Law (which instituted a national waiting period and the option of a police background check for handgun sales from licensed gun dealers) at its first year's anniversary (February 28, 1995) has raised some questions about its usefulness as a crime-fighting measure.

As noted by the NRA [National Rifle Association], a report issued by Attorney General Janet Reno showed the five-day national waiting period has netted only four federal prosecutions of prohibited persons attempting to purchase a firearm. Under the Clinton Administration, federal prosecutions of armed criminals have plummeted 23%.

MISSED THE BOAT

"This goes to show that while Bill Clinton is long on political rhetoric, he's missed the boat when it comes to crime-fighting," the NRA said in a bulletin.

While President Clinton has released information showing that in the first full year of the Law some 70,000 persons were prevented from buying handguns, the vast majority of those individuals initially identified as being prohibited from buying a gun under Brady were later found to be qualified.

Many have been misidentified or have had minor skirmishes with the law, such as not paying their parking tickets. The Bureau of Alcohol, Tobacco and Firearms (BATF) is alleged to be withholding the issuance of Federal Firearms Licenses (FFLs) to applicants found to have unpaid parking tickets. Federal law identifies those persons prohibited from purchasing firearms as convicted felons, fugitives from justice, illegal aliens, juveniles, those judged as being mentally ill and persons under a court restraining order as a result of a domestic violence complaint.

A PRO-GUN-CONTROL STUDY

On the other side of the coin, Handgun Control, Inc. (HCI) is trying to put as best a spin on the situation as possible to uphold its arguments in favor of the law. In a late-February 1995-issued memorandum to the nation's media, HCI released the results of a study entitled: "The Brady Law: One Year Proves Effectiveness." In a similar fashion, the anti-gun-oriented International Association of Chiefs of Police (IACP) and HCI conducted a study of 115 law enforcement jurisdictions in 27 states which had not been doing background checks.

The survey reveals that "3.34% (or 19,098 persons) of handgun purchasers (out of a total of 572,224 people) were denied weapons because of their background, largely because they were felons or had outstanding felony warrants against them. In Dougherty County in Georgia, for example, a sheriff reported 60 denials, including 15 because of felony warrants; 15 arrests were made."

CALIFORNIA HANDGUN WAITING PERIODS AND MURDER RATES

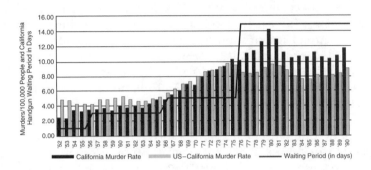

Clayton E. Cramer, *American Rifleman*, April 1993.

However, as the NRA revealed, very few prohibited individuals are being prosecuted for attempting to purchase guns. By HCI's own admission, the 15 arrests made in the Georgia county were based on outstanding felony warrants, not because the prohibited persons attempted to buy a firearm. One could wonder why the police were not more effective in arresting those 15 individuals who had outstanding arrest warrants issued against them long before they went to their local gun shops.

As to the other 45 denials in this Georgia county, no explanation was offered by HCI as to the reasons for the denial. Were there extenuating circumstances involved or did they just happen to have outstanding parking tickets? . . .

SURVEY BACKGROUND

When the Brady Law went into effect, 32 states which had not previously checked the backgrounds of handgun buyers were required to do so. (The other 18 states were already conducting their own checks through state laws.)

Author's Note: One reason the general media reports so many inaccuracies when it comes to firearms news is that it does not thoroughly check its sources of information. This was amply demonstrated by Susan Whitmore, HCI's director of communications, in a media memorandum on the survey in which she stated sev-

eral times that the Brady Law "requires" background checks of handgun buyers. This is simply not true as the law's language directs police to make a "reasonable effort" to conduct such checks.

THE BRADY STATES

The HCI/IACP survey includes data from 27 of the new "Brady States." Eight state agencies (Arizona, Arkansas, Colorado, Idaho, Kentucky, South Carolina, Utah and West Virginia) and 107 municipal police and county sheriff's departments participated in the survey. The agencies contacted were asked to furnish their most current information available on background checks conducted since February 28, 1994 (the effective date of the law). The reporting periods varied slightly by department, with some ending as early as December 31, 1994, and others as late as February 23, 1995.

The percentage of denials varied from jurisdiction to jurisdiction. According to the HCI/IACP survey, the areas with the lowest rate of denials, actually no denials, were Seabrook, NH, with 75 background checks conducted; Fayetteville, NC, with 8,218 checks; and Murfreesboro, TN, with 14 checks and no denials of gun purchase. The three highest denial rates were Fort Worth, TX, with 1,142 gun purchase denials or 14.06% out of 8,120 attempts; Shelbyville, TN, with 105 denials or 13.91% out of 755 attempts to purchase; and Dothan, AL, with 50 persons denied or 10% out of 500 attempted.

SHORT ON ANSWERS

Whitmore reports that in Amarillo, TX, 35 denials resulted in five arrests (according to the survey). And in Arizona since October 1, 1994, when that state's Department of Public Safety became responsible for the background checks, 30 arrests were made, based on outstanding felony warrants. However, she does not explain the reasons for the denials of the many other persons. For example, Phoenix, AZ, reported in the survey 869 denials out of 37,703 checks. Why were the over 800 persons denied? This question the survey does not answer. Nor does it explain why police suddenly need the Brady Law to take action on outstanding arrest warrants.

In closing, Whitmore stated that "the Brady Law was enacted to end the 'honor system' by which guns were sold over the counter, with no check of the buyer. It was never intended to, alone, solve the nation's gun violence problem. Certainly legislation is still needed to stem the illegal gun market, prevent thefts of guns, and stop widespread gun trafficking. But the Brady Law is a serious effort to stop the sale of handguns to criminals. One year later, it has proven effective at that charge," she said.

The author notes that the results of the survey prove just the opposite to him, as the overwhelming majority of the areas surveyed showed persons with clean backgrounds (without even so much as an overdue parking ticket) comprised the bulk of the purchasers from legitimate gun dealers.

"These [assault] weapons have no sporting purpose—they are eminently more suitable for combat with other humans than for hunting deer."

BANNING ASSAULT WEAPONS WILL REDUCE GUN VIOLENCE

Kenneth T. Lyons

Kenneth T. Lyons is the president of the International Brotherhood of Police Officers, the largest police union in the United States. The following viewpoint is excerpted from testimony Lyons gave at a Senate Judiciary Committee hearing in 1993. Lyons argues that semiautomatic assault weapons are the guns of choice of drug dealers and other criminals. These firearms have no legitimate purpose other than to kill people, he contends, and their very existence puts police officers and innocent bystanders at risk. A national ban on assault weapons is necessary, Lyons maintains, in order to protect law enforcement officials and law-abiding citizens from criminals who find it easy to buy the guns in states with lax gun-control laws. Congress banned the manufacture, sale, and possession of nineteen semiautomatic weapons in 1994.

As you read, consider the following questions:

1. What three reasons does Lyons give to justify banning semiautomatic assault weapons?
2. According to Lyons, what seven characteristics make a firearm unsuitable for sporting purposes?
3. What percentage of guns traced by the Bureau of Alcohol, Tobacco, and Firearms in 1990 and 1991 were assault weapons, according to the author?

Kenneth T. Lyons's testimony before the Senate Committee on the Judiciary, August 3, 1993.

In the 1930s, our country saw a dramatic increase in gangster activity, violence, and general lawlessness. It was a time when the mafia held all of the cards and the police were increasingly powerless to protect the innocents. One of the actions then taken by Congress was to severely restrict the purchase and transfer of machine guns, or fully automatic assault weapons. The result was a virtual elimination of machine guns within a few years.

In the 1990s, our country is once again seeing a dramatic increase in gangster activity, violence, and general lawlessness. Times, of course, have changed. Today's gangsters often wear sneakers rather than wing-tips, bandannas rather than pin-stripes, and deal drugs rather than alcohol. There is one thing, however, that the two brands of criminals have in common: their choice of high powered weapons of destruction.

ASSAULT WEAPONS SHOULD BE BANNED

Mr. Chairman [Joseph R. Biden Jr., chairman of the Senate Judiciary Committee], there are a number of reasons for taking strong, swift action to ban the sale, manufacture, and possession of semi-automatic assault weapons. First of all, police officers are in a particularly dangerous and demanding profession. Each year, approximately 150 officers are killed in the line of duty. For every one officer killed, another 150 are assaulted. The increased destructive possibilities of semi-automatic assault weapons increase the risk to those officers who put their lives on the line every day. Each traffic stop, each pursuit of a dangerous felon, each knock on a door to serve a warrant can end in disaster for the officer.

A second reason for banning semi-automatic assault weapons is that they can easily be converted from semi-automatic weapons into fully automatic weapons. Mr. Chairman, these weapons, such as the AK-47, were designed to be military weapons, and thus have increased firing capacity. Because fully automatic weapons are prohibited in this country, the manufacturers that produce assault weapons must design them to fire semi-automatic. However, the very design of these weapons makes it simple for criminals to convert them into fully automatic weapons, thus increasing their dangerous propensities.

NO SPORTING PURPOSE

As the Bureau of Alcohol, Tobacco, and Firearms determined prior to President George Bush's banning the importation of 43 types of assault weapons in 1989, these weapons have absolutely no legitimate sporting purpose. Mr. Chairman, our organization [the International Brotherhood of Police Officers] and our membership are in a good position to judge the debate on gun control. We are aware of the legitimate and illegitimate uses of firearms. Many of our members are hunters and sportsmen. Many of those same members tell us that these weapons have no legitimate sporting purpose.

©Britt/Copley News Service. Reprinted with permission.

For example, many of these weapons have the following characteristics:

- Folding stocks—which sacrifice accuracy for concealability and mobility—an advantage in combat but not in hunting deer;
- Shorter barrel length (less than 22 inches)—another facet which sacrifices accuracy for mobility in close combat;
- Pistol grips on rifles or shotguns—which allow the weapon to fire easily from the hip—great for spraying a crowd of people, but less effective for hunting deer;
- Threaded barrels—which allow an adaptable silencer to be attached, but there is no need for a silencer in the woods;
- Barrel mounts—designed to accommodate bayonets—great for hand-to-hand combat with humans, but not with deer and other game;
- Flash suppressor—an innovation designed to conceal the shooter's location at night—certainly serves no sporting purpose;
- Large capacity detachable magazine—which allows literally

hundreds of rounds in a few minutes. In contrast, standard hunting rifles are equipped with 3 or 4 shot magazines.

As you can see, Mr. Chairman, these weapons have no sporting purpose—they are eminently more suitable for combat with other humans than for hunting deer or other legitimate sporting purposes. Add these characteristics to the ease with which these weapons are convertible to fully automatic, and law enforcement is faced with a tremendously dangerous weapon.

LAW ENFORCEMENT AND HOLLYWOOD

One of the reasons that these weapons are turning up in increasing numbers on the street, and that these weapons have become the choice of drug dealers and criminals, is the frequency with which these weapons appear on the sets of Hollywood movies. Mr. Chairman, the glamour of violence on television and in the movies is having a debilitating effect on our children. Violence is glorified, and kids emulate what they see. In addition, I would assert that the proliferation of purportedly "realistic"television shows about police officers sends a dual message about law enforcement. One the one hand, a close look at these programs can result in increased respect for the difficult job that police officers do. On the other hand, these shows only reinforce the "cops and robbers" image of police, an image at odds with our goal of community-oriented policing—of the cop patrolling his or her community, rather than speeding down the street at 60 miles an hour in pursuit of a felon.

STATISTICS ON ASSAULT WEAPONS

Make no mistake about it, Mr. Chairman, assault weapons are the "in" weapon to protect one's turf from competing drug dealers. Don't be misled by the seemingly low number of assault weapons found in various surveys. The cop on the street is being outgunned. Many departments are upgrading their service weapons from .38 caliber revolvers to 9 mm semi-automatics because they are unable to keep up with the firepower which they are facing as criminals move to these assault weapons. Assault weapons make up about 1.5% to 3% of the guns in the country, but make up 7% of the guns which law enforcement asks ATF to trace. In 1991, 6.8% (3,683 of 53,924) of the firearms traced by ATF were assault weapons. In 1990, 7% (3,352 of 47,770) of the firearms traced by ATF were assault weapons.

We certainly can't afford to wait until the statistics go up before we take action to ban these weapons. According to the California Assembly Office of Research, 83% of more than 200 law enforcement agencies in California reported either a significant (63%) or moderate (20%) increase in both the type and frequency of use of assault weapons since the late 1980s. More than 65% of the respondents felt that assault weapons were either displacing pistols and revolvers as the weapon of choice (34%) or augmenting the firearms arsenal of gang members and offenders (32%). And while we hear the arguments that assault weapons cannot be defined or are similar to other firearms, we see cops, children, and innocent bystanders being shot and killed.

THE MOST SENSIBLE SOLUTION

Mr. Chairman, a national ban on assault weapons would prevent the circumstances that led to the tragic incident in San Francisco in July 1993 where a madman walked into a law firm, armed to the teeth, and killed eight people and seriously wounded six others. In this case, Gian Luigi Ferri purchased the TEC-DC9's across the California state line in Nevada—becoming one of many individuals who travel from one state into another to circumvent state laws which restrict the use and sale of such weapons. Such circumvention of laws is common—as we know many of the guns used for crime in New York and New England, states with strong gun control laws, come from states such as Virginia and Georgia, which have lax gun control laws. This is why a national ban is the most sensible solution.

| "Despite the scary-looking, military-style features, the ['assault'] guns are no more lethal than hundreds of firearms that remain legal."

BANNING ASSAULT WEAPONS WILL NOT REDUCE GUN VIOLENCE

Jacob Sullum

The congressional ban on the production and importation of "assault weapons" is based on faulty reasoning, argues Jacob Sullum in the following viewpoint. Contrary to popular belief, he maintains, semiautomatic "assault weapons" are no more deadly than other semiautomatic weapons. Since the firearms subject to the ban are rarely used to commit crimes, Sullum contends, banning them will do little to reduce gun violence. Sullum is a senior editor at *Reason* magazine, a periodical of libertarian social and political thought.

As you read, consider the following questions:

1. Who introduced the bill banning "assault weapons," according to the author?
2. How many types of firearms are covered under the ban, according to Sullum?
3. Why is the number of "assault weapons" traced by the Bureau of Alcohol, Tobacco, and Firearms each year not an accurate representation of the guns used in violent crime, according to David Kopel, as cited by Sullum?

Jacob Sullum, "Weapon Assault." Reprinted, with permission, from the July 1994 issue of *Reason* magazine. Copyright 1994 by the Reason Foundation, 3415 S. Sepulveda Blvd., Suite 400, Los Angeles, CA 90034.

S uppose a lobby group wants congress to ban "death cars." They are a little fuzzy about what, exactly, "death cars" are, but the vehicles seem to share certain characteristics, including red paint and speedometers that go above 100 mph. These cars are said to be the favored vehicles of speeders and drunk drivers, and they are supposedly designed to cause accidents that kill as many people as possible. Supporters of the ban cannot back up their claims with mechanical explanations or statistics, but they can provide the gruesome details of crashes involving "death cars."

WEAK ARGUMENTS

The logic behind the "assault weapon" ban approved by Congress in 1994 is hardly more compelling than the case against "death cars." The legislation's success says more about the level of contempt for the Second Amendment than it does about the strength of arguments for the ban.

Introduced by Sen. Dianne Feinstein (D-Calif.) and Rep. Charles Schumer (D-N.Y.), the "assault weapon" ban forbids making or importing ammunition clips holding more than 10 rounds and semiautomatic firearms that accept such clips and have two or more of these features: folding stock, pistol grip, bayonet mount, threaded barrel for a flash suppressor, grenade launch mount, barrel shroud. The law bans 19 firearms by name, but it covers a total of 184 current models, as well as any new guns that fit the definition.

Notwithstanding the claim by three former presidents that "this is a matter of vital importance to the public safety," there is little reason to believe that banning these weapons will have any effect on violent crime. Despite the scary-looking, military-style features, the guns are no more lethal than hundreds of firearms that remain legal. They fire at the same rate as any other semiautomatic gun—in other words, no faster than a revolver. Their ammunition is of intermediate caliber, less formidable than the cartridges fired by many hunting rifles.

Comments by members of Congress indicate widespread confusion about the capabilities of "assault weapons." Rep. Ronald D. Coleman (D-Tex.) said he reversed his opposition to the ban because he wanted to "make it harder for drug thugs and gangs to get the machine guns that wantonly kill our police officers and children." Rep. Henry Hyde (R-Ill.), whose much-publicized switch helped rescue the ban when it seemed headed for defeat, asked: "What's the difference between a hand grenade and an AK-47 that can spray a crowd and kill people?"

Despite the implication of these and other remarks by supporters of the ban, the legislation does not deal with machine guns, which are already severely restricted by federal law. Since even members of Congress who voted for the ban don't seem to know which guns it covers, the strong support for the measure among the general public does not mean much (although it does suggest that voting for the ban did not take quite as much "courage" as the gun-control lobby would have us believe).

A Shoddy Case

Supporters of the ban also argued that "assault weapons" are disproportionately represented among guns used in crimes. "Although assault weapons account for less than 1% of the guns in circulation," wrote former Presidents Gerald Ford, Jimmy Carter, and Ronald Reagan in a letter to House members, "they account for nearly 10 percent of the guns traced to crime." This number refers to weapons traced by the Bureau of Alcohol, Tobacco, and Firearms. But gun-control scholar David Kopel reports that the BATF traces less than 2 percent of the guns used in violent crime each year, and the sample is not representative.

Less than One-Quarter of 1 Percent

Since police started keeping statistics, we now know that assault weapons are or were used in an underwhelming 0.26 of 1 percent of crimes in New Jersey. Less than one-quarter of 1 percent of the crime in New Jersey was attributed to assault weapons. That is really nothing. This means that [police] officers are more likely to confront an escaped tiger from the local zoo than they are to confront one of these weapons.

Joseph Constance, Testimony before the Senate Judiciary Committee, August 3, 1993.

As Kopel notes, "assault weapons" are more likely to be traced than other guns precisely because they are unusual and have been the subject of so much attention. Furthermore, almost all of them were made after the Gun Control Act of 1968 and therefore have serial numbers, which are necessary to do a trace. Inventories of guns seized from criminals in major cities indicate that trace figures vastly overstate the use of "assault weapons" in crime. Summarizing data from 24 such inventories, criminologist Gary Kleck writes: "Virtually all of these studies show that only 0 to 4 percent of confiscated guns are assault weapons."

Because the statistics show that "assault weapons" are rarely used in crime, advocates of the ban tended to focus on specific cases. Handgun Control Inc. took out a full-page ad in the April 27, 1994, *New York Times* describing four murders committed with weapons or magazines covered by the ban. And Hyde said he decided to vote for the ban after Feinstein provided him with accounts of murders, including some in Chicago. This sort of appeal can have a strong emotional impact, but it carries no logical weight whatsoever. Handgun Control Inc. or Feinstein could just as easily have found examples of murders committed with shotguns or revolvers. The anecdotes proved nothing about the merits of the bill.

In the end, the shoddiness of the case for the "assault weapon" ban makes it all the more formidable as a precedent. Gun-control activists will use the points made by the ban's critics to argue for more-sweeping restrictions. They will note that the ban has not had an observable effect on crime. They will discover that it leaves untouched many guns that are just as dangerous as "assault weapons," if not more so. And they will already have established that it's OK to violate the right to keep and bear arms, as long as you have a reason. It doesn't even have to be a good one.

PERIODICAL BIBLIOGRAPHY

The following articles have been selected to supplement the diverse views presented in this chapter. Addresses are provided for periodicals not indexed in the *Readers' Guide to Periodical Literature*, the *Alternative Press Index*, the *Social Sciences Index*, or the *Index to Legal Periodicals and Books*.

Dianne Feinstein	"Is the Federal Ban on Assault Weapons Working?" *Insight*, February 26, 1996. Available from 3600 New York Ave. NE, Washington, DC 20002.
André Henderson	"Gun Control's Costly Ammunition," *Governing*, May 1994.
Christopher Hitchens	"Minority Report," *Nation*, January 24, 1994.
Vincent Lane	"Public Housing Sweep Stakes," *Policy Review*, Summer 1994.
John R. Lott Jr. and David B. Mustard	"Crime, Deterrence, and Right-to-Carry Concealed Handguns," *Journal of Legal Studies*, January 1997.
David McDowall, Colin Loftin, and Brian Wiersema	"Easing Concealed Firearms Laws: Effects on Homicides in Three States," *Journal of Criminal Law and Criminology*, Fall 1995.
Tom Morganthau	"Too Many Guns? Or Too Few?" *Newsweek*, August 15, 1994.
Nation	"Sweeps Week," May 9, 1994.
Josh Sugarmann and Kristen Rand	"Cease Fire," *Rolling Stone*, March 10, 1994.
Jacob Sullum	"Tactical Tragedies," *Reason*, March 1994.
Jacob Sullum	"Wait a Minute," *National Review*, February 7, 1994.
William R. Tonso	"Shooting Blind," *Reason*, November 1995.
Gordon Witkin	"New Support for Concealed Weapons," *U.S. News & World Report*, November 28, 1994.

FOR FURTHER DISCUSSION

CHAPTER 1

1. Claire Safran contends that a city's crime rate is directly influenced by the availability of handguns—Seattle's crime rate is high because handguns are easily obtained, and Vancouver's is low because handguns are difficult to obtain. Daniel D. Polsby maintains that during the days of the Wild West the crime rate was low because everyone was armed. Whose argument is more persuasive? Can you think of any other factors that may affect the crime rate? What are they?

2. Josh Sugarmann asserts that because thirty-seven thousand Americans die from gun-related violence each year, doctors have a right and a duty to consider such violence a public-health issue. Tucker Carlson contends that doctors misinterpret data to support their own conclusions about guns and gun violence. Whose argument is stronger? Why?

CHAPTER 2

1. J. Neil Schulman cites Roy Copperud, an expert in the usage of the English language, who interprets the Second Amendment to mean that an individual's right to own firearms cannot be restricted in any way. Chris Sprigman, an attorney, contends that several U.S. Supreme Court decisions allow restrictions to be placed on gun ownership by individuals. Based on your readings of the viewpoints, do you think individual gun ownership can be constitutionally restricted? Explain your answer.

2. The Los Angeles Times contends that the framers of the Second Amendment only intended to grant states the right to maintain militias. Steven Silver disputes this contention, arguing instead that the Second Amendment does not limit gun ownership to members of state militias. What evidence do the authors offer to support these arguments? In your opinion, how should the Second Amendment be interpreted? Defend your answer, using quotes from the viewpoints.

CHAPTER 3

1. Joel Rosenberg and Barbara L. Keller both offer personal accounts of home burglaries, yet they come to opposite conclusions about whether guns should be used for self-protection. Which argument do you find more persuasive? Why?

2. Gary Kleck and Marc Gertz maintain that the use of guns for self-defense is much more common than government surveys indicate. Garen J. Wintemute contends that the government's

National Crime Victimization Survey is an accurate measure of defensive gun use. Based on information from the viewpoints, what are the strengths and weaknesses of each study? Which do you think provides a more accurate measure of defensive gun use? Why?

3. When individuals are allowed to carry concealed weapons, David B. Kopel maintains, society as a whole is safer because criminals do not know who is armed and who is not. The Coalition to Stop Gun Violence contends that allowing individuals to carry concealed weapons would result in a more violent society. After reading the viewpoints, do you think individuals should be allowed to own and carry guns without any restrictions? Explain your answer.

CHAPTER 4

1. Before the Brady law (which requires a five-day waiting period and background checks on would-be handgun purchasers) went into effect in February 1994, most states used the honor system to prevent prohibited individuals from purchasing handguns. Robert Hausman maintains that too few prohibited persons are caught by the background checks to make the Brady law worthwhile. Do you agree with his argument that compliance with the Brady law requires more effort than it is worth? Why or why not?

2. Kenneth T. Lyons contends that assault weapons are a favorite weapon of criminals and that banning these firearms will reduce violent crime. Jacob Sullum maintains that these weapons are rarely used to commit crimes and therefore the ban will do little to reduce gun violence. Lyons is the president of the nation's largest police union. Sullum is an editor for *Reason*, a libertarian magazine. Does knowing the authors' occupations affect your assessment of their arguments? If so, how?

3. Gun-control proponents advocate a number of measures to reduce gun-related violence, including waiting periods, background checks, registering and licensing handgun owners, high taxes on ammunition, limiting the size of ammunition clips, and a total ban on certain firearms and bullets. Opponents of gun control contend that any restrictions on firearms, ammunition, and gun ownership would be ineffective against reducing gun crime, would lead to more severe restrictions, and would violate their constitutional rights. Based on your reading of the viewpoints in this book, what measures, if any, do you think should be imposed on guns, ammunition, or gun owners? Support your answer with examples from the viewpoints.

Organizations to Contact

The editors have compiled the following list of organizations concerned with the issues debated in this book. The descriptions are derived from materials provided by the organizations. All have publications or information available for interested readers. The list was compiled on the date of publication of the present volume; names, addresses, phone and fax numbers, and e-mail/Internet addresses may change. Be aware that many organizations take several weeks or longer to respond to inquiries, so allow as much time as possible.

American Civil Liberties Union (ACLU)
132 W. 43rd St., New York, NY 10036
(212) 944-9800 • fax: (212) 869-9065
The ACLU champions the rights set forth in the Declaration of Independence and the U.S. Constitution. It opposes the suppression of individual rights. The ACLU interprets the Second Amendment as a guarantee for states to form militias, not as a guarantee of the individual right to own and bear firearms. Consequently, the organization believes that gun control is constitutional and that because guns are dangerous, gun control is necessary. The ACLU publishes the semiannual *Civil Liberties* in addition to policy statements and reports.

Citizens Committee for the Right to Keep and Bear Arms
12500 NE Tenth Pl., Bellevue, WA 98005
(206) 454-4911 • fax: (206) 451-3959
The committee believes that the U.S. Constitution's Second Amendment guarantees and protects the right of individual Americans to own guns. It works to educate the public concerning this right and to lobby legislators to prevent the passage of gun-control laws. The committee is affiliated with the **Second Amendment Foundation** and has more than six hundred thousand members. It publishes the books *Gun Laws of America*, *Gun Rights Fact Book*, *Origin of the Second Amendment*, and *Point Blank: Guns and Violence in America*.

Coalition to Stop Gun Violence
1000 16th St. NW, Suite 603, Washington, DC 20036-5705
(202) 530-0340 • fax: (202) 530-0331
e-mail: noguns@aol.com • Internet: http://www.gunfree.inter.net
Formerly the National Coalition to Ban Handguns, the coalition lobbies at the local, state, and federal levels to ban the sale of handguns and assault weapons to individuals. It also litigates cases against firearms makers. Its publications include various informational sheets on gun violence and the papers "Overrated: The NRA's Role in the 1994 Elections" and "The Unspoken Tragedy: Firearm Suicide in the United States."

Doctors for Integrity in Policy Research (DIPR)

5201 Norris Canyon Rd., Suite 140, San Ramon, CA 94583
(510) 277-0333 • fax: (510) 820-5118
e-mail: EdgarSuter@aol.com

DIPR is a national think tank of approximately five hundred medical school professors, researchers, and practicing physicians who are committed to exposing biased and incompetent research, editorial censorship, and unsound public policy. It believes that substandard science is extremely prevalent in medical literature on guns and violence. DIPR publishes the papers "Guns in Medical Literature: A Failure of Peer Review," "'Assault Weapons' Revisited: An Analysis of the AMA Report," and "Gun Control Revisited: Religion or Science?"

Educational Fund to End Handgun Violence

1000 16th St. NW, Suite 603, Washington, DC 20036-5705
(202) 530-5888 • fax: (202) 530-0331
e-mail: edfund@aol.com • Internet: http://www.gunfree.inter.net

The fund is a nonprofit educational charity dedicated to ending gun violence, especially violence against children. It provides information concerning handgun violence, firearms marketing and production, and firearm design. The fund sponsors educational programs and publishes the quarterly newsletter *Firearm Litigation Reporter*, the manual *Grass Roots Organizing*, and the booklet *Kids and Guns: A National Disgrace*.

Handgun Control, Inc.

1225 Eye St. NW, Suite 1100, Washington, DC 20005
(202) 898-0792 • fax: (202) 371-9615

A citizens lobby working for the federal regulation of the manufacture, sale, and civilian possession of handguns and automatic weapons, the organization successfully promoted the passage of the Brady law, which mandates a five-day waiting period for the purchase of handguns. The lobby publishes the quarterly newsletter *Progress Report* and the book *Guns Don't Die—People Do*, as well as legislative reports and pamphlets.

Independence Institute

14142 Denver West Pkwy., Suite 101, Golden, CO 80401
(303) 279-6536 • fax: (303) 279-4176

The Independence Institute is a pro–free market think tank that supports gun ownership as a civil liberty and a constitutional right. Its publications include books and booklets opposing gun control, such as *Children and Guns: Sensible Solutions*, *The Assault Weapon Panic: "Political Correctness" Takes Aim at the Constitution*, and *The Samurai, the Mountie, and the Cowboy*.

Jews for the Preservation of Firearms Ownership (JPFO)

2872 S. Wentworth Ave., Milwaukee, WI 53207
(414) 769-0760 • fax: (414) 483-8435

JPFO is an educational organization that believes Jewish law mandates self-defense. Its primary goal is the elimination of the idea that gun control is a socially useful public policy in any country. JPFO publishes the quarterly *Firearms Sentinel*, the comic book *"Gun Control" Kills Kids!*, and the books *Gun Control: Gateway to Tyranny* and *Lethal Laws*.

The Lawyer's Second Amendment Society
18034 Ventura Blvd., No. 329, Encino, CA 91316
(818) 734-3066
e-mail: rkbaesq@ix.netcom.com

The society is a nationwide network of attorneys and others who are interested in preserving the right to keep and bear arms. It attempts to educate citizens about what it believes is their inalienable right, provided by the Constitution's framers, to defend themselves with firearms, if necessary. The society publishes the *Firearms Sentinel* quarterly and the *Liberty Poll* newsletter six times a year.

National Crime Prevention Council (NCPC)
Information Services, 1700 K St. NW, 2nd Fl., Washington, DC 20006
(202) 466-6272 • fax: (202) 296-1356

The NCPC is a branch of the U.S. Department of Justice. It works to teach Americans how to reduce crime and addresses the causes of crime in its programs and educational materials. It provides readers with information on gun control and gun violence. The NCPC's publications include the newsletter *Catalyst*, which is published ten times a year, the book *Reducing Gun Violence: What Communities Can Do*, and the booklet *Making Children, Families, and Communities Safer from Violence*.

National Rifle Association of America (NRA)
11250 Waples Mill Rd., Fairfax, VA 22030
(703) 267-1000 • fax: (703) 267-3989
Internet: http://www.nra.org

The NRA, with nearly three million members, is America's largest organization of gun owners. It is the primary lobbying group for those who oppose gun control laws. The NRA believes that such laws violate the U.S. Constitution and do nothing to reduce crime. In addition to its monthly magazines *American Rifleman*, *American Hunter*, and *Incites*, the NRA publishes numerous books, bibliographies, reports, and pamphlets on gun ownership, gun safety, and gun control.

Second Amendment Foundation
12500 NE Tenth Pl., Bellevue, WA 98005
(206) 454-7012 • fax: (206) 451-3959

The foundation is dedicated to informing Americans about their Second Amendment right to keep and bear firearms. It believes that gun-control laws violate this right. The foundation publishes the quarterly newsletters *Second Amendment Reporter* and *Gottleib/Tartaro Report* and the magazines *Gun Week* and *Women and Guns*.

Violence Policy Center

2000 P St. NW, Suite 200, Washington, DC 20036

(202) 822-8200 • fax: (202) 822-8205

The center is an educational foundation that conducts research on fire-arms violence. It works to educate the public concerning the dangers of guns and supports gun-control measures. The center's publications include the report "Cease Fire: A Comprehensive Strategy to Reduce Firearms Violence" and the books NRA: *Money, Firepower, and Fear* and *Assault Weapons and Accessories in America*.

BIBLIOGRAPHY OF BOOKS

Jack Anderson — *Inside the NRA: Armed and Dangerous: An Exposé*. New York: Dove, 1996.

Robert J. Cottrol, ed. — *Gun Control and the Constitution: Sources and Explorations on the Second Amendment*. New York: Garland, 1994.

Osha Gray Davidson — *Under Fire: The NRA and the Battle for Gun Control*. New York: Henry Holt, 1993.

Wilbur Edel — *Gun Control: Threat to Liberty or Defense Against Anarchy?* Westport, CT: Praeger, 1995.

Susan Glick — *Female Persuasion: A Study of How the Firearms Industry Markets to Women and the Reality of Women and Guns*. Washington, DC: Violence Policy Center, 1994.

Ted Gottfried — *Gun Control: Public Safety and the Right to Bear Arms*. Brookfield, CT: Millbrook, 1993.

Alan Gottlieb — *The Gun Grabbers*. Bellevue, WA: Merril, 1994.

Dennis A. Henigan, E. Bruce Nicholson, and David Hemenway — *Guns and the Constitution: The Myth of Second Amendment Protection for Firearms in America*. Northampton, MA: Aletheia Press, 1995.

Donald D. Hook — *Gun Control: The Continuing Debate*. Bellevue, WA: Second Amendment Foundation, 1993.

Gary Kleck — *Point Blank: Guns and Violence in America*. New York: Aldine de Gruyter, 1991.

David B. Kopel — *The Samurai, the Mountie, and the Cowboy: Should America Adopt the Gun Controls of Other Democracies?* Buffalo: Prometheus, 1992.

David B. Kopel, ed. — *Guns: Who Should Have Them?* Amherst, NY: Prometheus, 1995.

Earl R. Kruschke — *Gun Control: A Reference Handbook*. Santa Barbara, CA: ABC-Clio, 1995.

Wayne LaPierre — *Guns, Crime, and Freedom*. Washington, DC: Regnery, 1994.

Erik Larson — *Lethal Passage: How the Travels of a Single Handgun Expose the Roots of America's Gun Crisis*. New York: Crown, 1994.

Joyce Lee Malcolm — *To Keep and Bear Arms: The Origins of an Anglo-American Right*. Cambridge, MA: Harvard University Press, 1994.

Gary Mauser — *Gun Control Is Not Crime Control*. Vancouver, BC: Fraser Institute, 1995.

J. Neil Schulman   *Stopping Power: Why Seventy Million Americans Own Guns.*
                                Santa Monica, CA: Synapse-Centurion, 1994.

Joseph F. Sheley   *In the Line of Fire: Youths, Guns, and Violence in Urban*
and James D. Wright   *America.* New York: Aldine de Gruyter, 1995.

Robert J. Spitzer   *The Politics of Gun Control.* Chatham, NJ: Chatham
                               House, 1995.

Josh Sugarmann   *National Rifle Association: Money, Firepower, and Fear.*
                               Washington, DC: National Press Books, 1992.

James D. Wright and   *Armed and Considered Dangerous: A Survey of Felons and*
Peter H. Rossi   *Their Firearms.* New York: Aldine de Gruyter, 1994.

Franklin E. Zimring   *The Citizen's Guide to Gun Control.* New York:
and Gordon Hawkins   Macmillan, 1992.

INDEX

149
Fieldstein, Jill, 152
firearms industry
  lack of regulatory oversight
    of, 51, 52-53
Ford, Gerald, 169
Freeh, Louis J., 148

Gallup polls
  on household gun
    ownership, 113
  on waiting period for
    handgun purchase, 38
General Accounting Office,
  U.S.
  study on gun accidents, 71
Gerson, Stewart, 67
Gertz, Marc, 108
Graham, Bob, 125
gun control
  debate in United States over,
    24
  eligibility vs. restrictive
    permit systems, 40
  fosters misuse of firearms,
    69
  is public health issue, 53-54
    con, 56-61
  organizations supporting, 37
  police support for, 47, 49
  public support for, 25, 37
  puts potential victims at
    disadvantage, 31-32
Gun Control (Kukla), 146
Gun Control Act (1968), 38,
  169
Gun Owners, 149
guns
  carried by high school
    students, 118
  concealed. See concealed-
    carry laws
  defensive use of
    costs vs. benefits of, 120-21

estimates of, 115-16, 133
  are inconsistent, 109
incidents
  1988-1993, 112
  by victim-offender
    relationship, 1987-1990,
    122
  is underreported, 114-15
  in U.S., 1988-1993, 112
do not elicit aggression, 45
in home, likelihood of
  causing death in family, 23,
  41
gun safety training does not
  modify, 121
is increased by "weapons
  effect," 135
is overstated, 57-58
injuries from, 23
  economic costs of, 52
international comparisons of
  use of
  firearm fatalities, 22, 140
  problems with, 24-25
machine, ban on, 163
outright ban on
  constitutionality of, 86
private ownership
  encouraging would
    enhance security, 32-33
  has no relevance to
    maintaining state militia,
    95-96
Gurr, Ted Robert, 45

Hamilton, Alexander
  on purpose of Second
    Amendment, 81
Hammer, Marion, 126
Handgun Control, Inc., 60,
  153, 155
  support for Brady bill, 37-38
handguns
  are unsuitable for military